W9-DHT-278

DATE DUE

PUBLIC ORDER AND POPULAR DISTURBANCES

1660–1714

Public Order
and
Popular Disturbances

1660–1714

MAX BELOFF

FRANK CASS & CO LTD

1963

This edition published by
Frank Cass & Co. Ltd, 10 Woburn Walk,
London W.C. 1, by arrangement with
Oxford University Press.

63_24321

First published 1938
New impression 1963

Printed by Thomas Nelson (Printers) Ltd
London and Edinburgh

PREFACE

TO Professor G. N. Clark, who suggested the subject of this book and who gave me constant help and encouragement, I owe a debt of gratitude the reality of which only his pupils, perhaps, can adequately appreciate.

I wish to thank the Presidents and Fellows of the two learned foundations whose names appear on the title-page, to whom I owe the leisure which enabled me to pursue these researches.

The Clerks of the Peace of Oxfordshire and Northamptonshire and of the County Palatine of Chester kindly allowed me to see records in their custody, and Mr. J. C. Dewhurst, keeper of the records at Chester Castle, and Mr. R. B. Pugh of the Public Record Office were very helpful in many ways.

I should like to record the names of those friends who read and criticized the manuscript: Miss M. Coate, Dr. G. J. Renier, Mr. P. D. Whitting, Mr. K. E. Robinson, Miss O. M. Corthorn, and Mr. H. C. Seigal.

Miss Rachel Hoare and Mr. John Prestwich indefatigably read drafts and proofs, and I thank them both most sincerely.

To my mother, my first teacher, this book is affectionately dedicated.

M. B.
1938

CONTENTS

ABBREVIATIONS

THE following abbreviations have been used:

MANUSCRIPT SOURCES

(*a*) IN THE PUBLIC RECORD OFFICE.

P.C. 2. The Register of the Privy Council. (P.C. 2.)

S.P. Dom., King William's Chest. The Collection of State Papers called King William's Chest. (S.P. 8.)

C.S.P. Dom., Anne, MS. The Calendar of State Papers Domestic for the reign of Queen Anne. (Lit. Search Room, Press 2, no. 88.) (This calendar is unreliable, as the papers have been several times rearranged.)

State Papers Anne. The State Papers Domestic for the reign of Queen Anne. (S.P. 34.)

P.R.O. Assizes, 5. 13. The Records of the Clerks of Assize: Western Circuit Indictments, 1693. (Assizes 5. 13.)

(*b*) LOCAL RECORDS.

Cheshire County Records. The County Records in Chester Castle, Sessions Books and Rolls.

Northamptonshire Sessions Records. Sessions Books and Rolls in the County Hall, Northampton.

Oxfordshire Lieutenancy Papers. A bundle of papers relating to the Oxfordshire Lieutenancy in the County Hall, Oxford.

PRINTED SOURCES

C.S.P. Dom. and *C.S.P. Dom., Anne. The Calendars of State Papers, Domestic Series.*

C.S.P. Ven. The Calendars of State Papers, Venetian Series.

C.J. Journals of the House of Commons.

L.J. Journals of the House of Lords.

Stats. of Realm. *The Statutes of the Realm.* (London, 1810–22.)

Crawford. *Tudor and Stuart Proclamations, 1485–1714,* vol. i, England and Wales, ed. R. R. Steele. (Oxford, 1910.)

State Trials. A Complete Collection of State Trials. (London, 1730–66.)

H.M.C. The Reports of the Historical Manuscripts Commission.

Luttrell. Narcissus Luttrell, *A Brief Historical Relation of State Affairs.* 6 vols. (1857.)

Macaulay. *The History of England*, by Lord Macaulay. Edition in 6 vols. (1906.)

E.H.R. The English Historical Review.

V.C.H. The Victoria History of the Counties of England.

T.R.H.S. Transactions of the Royal Historical Society.

NOTES. (i) Owing to the methods adopted by the editors of the Calendars of State Papers, of some local records, and of the publications of the Historical MSS. Commission, it is not always possible to tell whether the matter printed is or is not a direct transcript from the original. Quotations from such sources must be read with this reservation.

(ii) The matter dealt with being purely domestic, the old-style dating has been used throughout, but the year has been taken to begin on the first of January.

INTRODUCTION

IN the following pages an attempt has been made to give an account of the major breaches of public order which occurred between the Restoration and the death of the last monarch of the House of Stuart. The causes of such disturbances have, where possible, been indicated and the machinery used for their suppression and for the maintenance of the peace briefly described.

The political side of such disturbances has been dealt with in as cursory a manner as possible. It has not been found necessary to do much more than refer to Monmouth's rebellion or the Revolution of 1688–9. Except, indeed, where they affected or were affected by social conditions, the political and religious conflicts of the time have been taken rather as the implied background of the subject than as one of its main constituents. The inclusion of the one chapter dealing with these matters has nevertheless helped to illustrate the administrative issues involved in the suppression of any type of disorder. And it further seemed only right that the historian should give some weight to what was clearly the primary preoccupation of the statesmen of the time.

One cannot pretend that the popular disturbances of this period are of great intrinsic interest or rich in dramatic appeal. Even the Sacheverell episode is chiefly of interest in that it foreshadows the darker terror which swept over the capital in 1780. As far as England outside the metropolitan area is concerned one is tempted to agree with the final judgement passed upon the first half of the eighteenth century by the historians of English local government:

'the impression of the country districts that we derive from many contemporary sources is that of a stolid, home-keeping and reasonably contented population; gross and sensual in its habits, but not incited to plunder or riot by extreme want; inclined occasionally to riot in resentment of this or that grievance, but saved by generous poor-relief from destitution and intellectually submissive to the justices of the peace.'[1]

[1] S. and B. Webb, *English Local Government: Statutory Authorities for Special Purposes*, 1922, p. 410.

It is, however, to be remembered that the authors of this passage are concerned primarily with drawing a contrast between the placidity of these periods and the darker colours in which they, and others of the same school, have painted the second half of the century and the early years of the succeeding one. Valuable as is their work, as marking the only attempt on a large scale to free eighteenth-century English history from its bondage to the writers of memoirs and the compilers of diplomatic dispatches, it is dominated in its turn by the authors' prime problem, the investigation of how changing economic and social circumstances made inevitable the supersession of the old system, or lack of system, in county and municipal government. This forward view has led, as it must lead, to a certain distortion of the earlier period dealt with. It is otherwise impossible to explain such a sentence as the following: 'At the outset of our analysis appears not any ancient principle but a new policy arising with dramatic suddenness out of the Revolution of 1689.'[1]

It is clear that neither in local government nor in the social structure of the country on which, in the last analysis, a system of local government must be based, does the Revolution of 1688–9 mark a dramatic break with the past. The system of *laissez-faire*, in regard not merely to the local administration of social policy but to social policy as a whole, dates not to the Revolution but to the dislocation of the central government caused by the Civil War and Interregnum, and to the final establishment of what is the key to English policy, external and internal, for a century and a half after 1660, 'The essential harmony that existed between the squirearchy and the rising industrial interests'.[2] An independent social policy on the part of the central government was—and the question of its former effectiveness is not hereby prejudiced—among the things that the Restoration failed to restore.[3]

It is this fact and also the existence in the half-century

---

[1] S. and B. Webb, p. 351. To this widespread tendency a notable exception is D. George, *London Life in the Eighteenth Century*, 1925.

[2] J. D. Chambers, *Nottinghamshire in the Eighteenth Century*, 1932, p. vi.

[3] Cf. E. Lipson, *Economic History of England*, 1931, iii. 264–5, 312–13, and 318.

which we are to examine of certain disquieting symptoms of social malaise, unnoticed or unemphasized by Mr. and Mrs. Webb, which make it worth while to re-examine their thesis, and to ask whether the comparative lack of popular disorder and, still more, the intellectual submissiveness to the justices of the peace are not suggestive of something other than universal content. One asks whether there was not, in fact, some popular reaction against the policies and methods of the ruling classes, who were themselves throughout the period to increase, at a pace hitherto unparalleled, both their own wealth and the national power, as that concept was understood in the age of mercantilism. And, further, one may ask whether, if such reaction is found to be comparatively weak, this fact is not due merely to the uneven balance of forces between the possessing classes and the discontented. It is well known that the period immediately following upon the Restoration saw changes of far-reaching social importance, expressed both in legislation and in administrative practice—changes which expressed the new balance of classes and the new temper of economic and social thought. The shift in the incidence of taxation, the granting of large-scale protection to industry and agriculture culminating in the corn-bounty, the continuance of the onslaught on the common lands, the reinforcement by the Act of Settlement of the old restrictions on the free movement of the labouring population are at least as important as the abandonment of serious attempts at enforcing medieval doctrines of fair wages and the fair price, which coincided with the relinquishing by the church for the first time of all responsibility for the ethics of economic practice.[1] 'The economic drift of the century', as Dr. Feiling has taught us, 'was towards a sharper demarcation of classes and towards depriving the poor of such economic protection as the Tudor and early Stuart governments had managed to keep up for them.'[2]

[1] For an excellent analysis of these changes see E. Wingfield-Stratford's *History of British Civilization*, 2nd ed., 1930, especially pp. 577–8. He possibly overemphasizes, however, the evils of the Act of Settlement when he says that it was 'in effect a reinstitution of villeinage without any of the advantages of seignorial protection and the custom of the manor'. On this subject see *infra*, Chap. II.

[2] K. Feiling, *History of the Tory Party*, 1924, p. 20.

We must remember, too, in assessing our slender evidence for the effect of these changes upon the daily lives of the masses of the people who were excluded from the ruling oligarchy, that passive acceptance of changes making for their economic disadvantage was by no means traditional in rural England. The Peasants' Revolt of 1381, the great rebellions of 1536 and 1549 had not merely been part of an active resistance to such changes, but had carried within them seeds of changes far more revolutionary than those which the peasant armies opposed. Their leaders, at least, unless we are wholly to discount the evidence of their opponents, were animated by a spirit of criticism of the whole social order which appeared responsible for the evils under which they laboured. Even the peasants of the seventeenth century, though the record of their sufferings and struggles has found as yet no Réville and no Tawney, had proved capable in its early years of a staunch struggle against the enclosure of the common lands, which in the Fen country, at least, lasted, as we shall see, well into the post-Restoration period.[1] In the great upheaval of the Civil War the communistic ideas which had so often made spasmodic appearances at times of great popular excitement came for a brief period to occupy a considerable place in the political and social controversy.[2] It is thus not unnatural to seek in the records of peasant or working-class disturbances some echo at least of these revolutionary aspirations.

If, however, we look at the England which emerged out of the changes of this period, the England of the Augustan age, whose constitution and social order were held a model to less happier lands, the England whose intellectual and political life is in some ways so near and familiar, we find, as many historians have reminded us, that one of its most remarkable features is the lack of class-feeling—a feeling of antagonism between rich and poor, which had, as we know, existed and was to exist again in a bitterer and more wide-spread form among the new proletariat of the industrial revolution.

[1] On the enclosure riots of the early years of the century see Lipson, ii. 400–4. For the fenmen see Chap. IV, *infra*.

[2] For the social reformers of the Interregnum see E. Bernstein, *Cromwell and Communism*, and G. P. Gooch, *English Democratic Ideas in the Seventeenth Century* (2nd ed., edited by H. J. Laski, 1927), chap. vii.

It has been rightly asserted that the riots of the eighteenth century were 'almost exclusively the mere impulse of an untamed people', 'mob outrages on a large scale excited by some local and temporary grievance', that there was in these riots 'no intermixture of sedition'.[1] Whether or no we agree with Professor G. M. Trevelyan that it was 'a national solidarity and unity of idea which bound Englishmen of all classes together', it would be difficult to dispute his opinion that, despite the undue concentration of power into the hands of one class and the uneven distribution of the national wealth, 'there was little or no social discontent'.[2] This apparent apathy of the eighteenth-century working-class is a cardinal fact to remember when we push back our researches into the previous age. 'Interpret it as we will, it is one of the strangest and most suggestive phenomena of our history.'[3]

In dealing with a period such as this, the primary difficulty of finding material is the most important of those confronting the social historian. The lower classes of society had not yet become articulate through the development of their own organizations and their own press. 'In those days philanthropists did not yet regard it as a sacred duty, nor had demagogues yet found it a lucrative trade to expatiate on the distress of the labourer. History was too much occupied with court and camp to spare a line for the hut of the peasant or the garret of the mechanic.'[4] It is therefore necessary to approach the history of these classes through the record of their overt acts—a record which can painfully be pieced together from legal and administrative sources and from stray references in news-letters and in private diaries and correspondence.

Such a method has at best but limited possibilities. By concentrating our attention upon discontent as manifested in disturbances, it invites us to neglect many of the real achievements of the age. It necessitates a constant watchfulness against the danger which always awaits the social

[1] S. and B. Webb, pp. 412–13.
[2] G. M. Trevelyan, 'The Age of Johnson' (from *Johnson's England*, ed. A. S. Turberville, 1933), p. 7.
[3] Wingfield-Stratford, p. 579.   [4] Macaulay, *History of England*, i. 433.

historian, that of exaggerating the evils of the particular period with which he is dealing. Much of the difficulty which we experience when trying to get into perspective the social history of modern England as a whole arises from this tendency. For the process of denigration has been applied successively to different periods, without any attempt being made to relate the particular evils presented to the general development of society.

In dealing with the later Stuart period one is fortunate at least in this respect, that the general history of the period is firmly imprinted on our minds through the literary genius of its great delineators. In the development of constitutional and religious liberties, in military glory and colonial expansion, in economic enterprise and organization, in literature and art, it is an age pre-eminent in British history. To deny that this is so would be foolish and is not the object of these pages. At the most, they give some indication of the price paid for these achievements by certain sections of the population and raise again the question, which is general as well as particular in its implications, as to how far the price was a necessary one.

For convenience in treatment—since a strict chronological account would over so short a period have served little purpose—a scheme of arrangement by subject has of necessity been adopted. It has resulted in the emergence of seven chapters. The first is an attempt to summarize the social conditions of the time and more especially those which had some bearing on the frequency of popular disorders. In the second, the disorders arising from religious and party conflict have been outlined. The next three are devoted to disturbances arising out of defects in the economic and fiscal systems. The position of the armed forces in relation to the general population is the theme of the sixth chapter, and, finally, the last chapter contains an account of the machinery of order and of its actual employment in this period.

These divisions are, however, largely formal. The popular discontents of the time cannot be understood unless they are related to the whole complex of changes which were then affecting English society. The measures taken to deal with the disorders and to prevent their recurrence are equally incomprehensible without some knowledge of the prevalent attitude to social and administrative problems. For this attitude the social changes of which we have spoken were no doubt in part responsible. But almost equally important was a set of opinions and prejudices, traditional in the society of the time, but rooted in the very different circumstances of the past. Thus is to be explained what may seem the most surprising of the phenomena revealed in the following chapters, the marked predominance which the mere repression of disorder maintained over the alleviation of distress.

I

SOCIAL ENGLAND, 1660–1714

THE turbulence of the lower orders in the England of the late seventeenth and early eighteenth centuries did not pass unnoticed by contemporaries. Even the history of the language bears witness to this. For it was at this time that the word 'mobile', or its contraction 'mob', came into general use to describe a disorderly gathering or even, in London at least, the lower classes as a whole. The protests of those who like Swift objected to the neologism and insisted on the older word 'rabble' were apparently unheeded.[1]

'The English', wrote Edward Chamberlayne, in the 1702 edition of his *Angliae Notitia*, 'differ from one another in their Humours, as they do in their Birth, Education and Profession. The Nobility, Gentry and Scholars, as well as most of the Merchants and chief Tradesmen are extreamly well polished in their behaviour; but the common sort are rude and even barbarous, as the effects of popular Tumults (which are here called the Mobile) shews, who when they are got together, commit the greatest outrages and render themselves sometimes very formidable, even to the Magistrate, who needs great Courage and Virtue to oppose them.'

It is hard to resist quoting the remainder of the passage:

'And here I would give the Reader one wholesome Caution, to wit that if ever he happens to fall under the displeasure of the Mobile in a Tumult, that he doth not vim vi repellere oppose 'em by Force, but by kind Words, pitiable Harangues, Condescensions or some such resigning Method get free from 'em and leave them to themselves; for he who treats them so divides them, and hereupon they generally fall out one among another.'[2]

There is, however, in these years nothing spectacular about the outbreaks of popular disorder. The rapidly increasing wealth of the country as a whole threw into harsh relief the great hardships suffered by certain sections, at least, of the working-class population.[3] The paternalism of the Elizabethan and early Stuart administration was replaced

---

[1] *The Spectator*, no. cxxxv; Swift, *Works*, ed. Temple Scott, ix. 35, n.

[2] *Angliae Notitia*, 20th ed., 1702, pp. 318–19.

[3] The growth of the nation's wealth in this period can be illustrated in many ways. William III's wars only provided a temporary setback to the increase in the number of new commercial and industrial enterprises and to rapid expansion of

by a social code harsher in theory and practice.[1] There is, nevertheless, no trace whatever of any mass movement for the bettering of working-class conditions, nor is there any trace of the survival or emergence among this class of social-revolutionary theories comparable with those which appear to have animated the medieval peasant risings, the anti-enclosure rebellions of the Tudor period, or the even more recent communistic movements of the Commonwealth period. The political and social aims of the once formidable Levellers seem indeed to have been forgotten very soon after the Restoration. The Venetian emissaries who reported on the state of England after a visit in the autumn of 1661 include Levellers along with Anabaptists, Brownists, Quakers, and others in a list of 'sectaries', that is to say of 'people all governed by their own fantasies who claim to have the spirit of God'.[2]

No doubt the inarticulacy of a largely illiterate class might have prevented literary form being given to such aspirations even had they existed, though there have been few revolutionary movements without prophets. But had such aspirations existed there can be little doubt that they would have been recorded by the defenders of the existing order, if only as one more proof of the incorrigible idleness and debauchery of the poor. In an age prolific in economic and social pamphleteering no considerable body of thought is likely wholly to have been neglected. As for the political theorists of the period, a glance at Locke is sufficient to show how far the fashionable apologists of the whig revolution were from the notion that social inequalities might possibly be held to affect the nature of the social bond.

There are to be found, it is true, occasional localized expressions of alarm due to the weakness of the civil administration in face of any riotous mob, however con-

the volume of foreign trade and of shipping. See Sir Charles Firth's reconsideration of Macaulay's third chapter in *History*, vol. xvii, 1932.

[1] The criticisms which have been levelled against an over-optimistic view of the social policy of the 'Eleven Years' Tyranny' may well be justified. But a comparison of the material collected in E. M. Leonard's *Early History of English Poor Relief* (1900) with the State Papers of our period is from this point of view striking enough, in default of further detailed research, to warrant the above remark.

[2] *C.S.P. Ven., 1661–4*, p. 86.

temptible its strength. But proposals for social reform, made by such writers as Pollexfen, are invariably backed by appeals to the pockets rather than to the fears of their wealthy readers. The major incentive to such speculation was the paradox of a rising poor-rate at a time of growing prosperity. In 1685 the total poor-rate of England was estimated at £665,000. By 1701 it had risen to £900,000.[1] But what was approached as an economic problem was explained in non-economic terms. Laziness rather than want of employment was more and more becoming the accepted explanation of working-class distress, and Defoe sounded a strangely modern note when he argued in his *Giving Alms no Charity*, in 1704, that if there were real want recruiting would not be so hard.

Two prominent figures deserve mention here as having viewed with less equanimity the growing impoverishment of large sections of the population. The Rev. Richard Baxter's *Poor Husbandman's Advocate* appealed to the landlords to lighten the burdens of the small tenant farmers, who were being increasingly subjected to rack-renting. Though his approach is essentially a religious one, and though he continually disclaims any 'levelling' principles, he warns his readers of the possible consequences of a neglect of his appeal. He recalls the horrors of the Peasants' Revolt in Germany and declares that it is those who oppress the people who will be responsible for 'Democracy or Anarchy'.[2] That such a possibility was even hinted at may explain why the treatise in which it occurs, the last he wrote, was not printed among his other posthumous works.

Still more significant are some remarks of John Bellers in the dedication to his *Essays about the Poor, Manufactures, Trade, Plantations and Immorality and of the Excellence and Divinity of Inward Light*. Writing in 1699, he calls attention to the recent rioting of the London silk-weavers against the importation of East India silks, and to the corn-riots which had taken place in various parts of the country. The needy of one trade had dared to brave Parliament; attacks on 'single Gentlemen at their own house' would not need so much hardihood. 'Foreign Wars waste our Treasure but

[1] Firth, loc. cit., p. 208.
[2] The Rev. Richard Baxter's last treatise, edited by F. J. Powicke, 1924.

Tumults at home are a Convulsion upon our Nerves: and though fines will awe Men of Estate, and Corporal Pains Men in Health: but (if Provision should fail) what can awe the Misery of Starving added to their increasing Immoralities which will increase their Insolence?'[1] If we discount the conventional reference to increasing immoralities this is a clear description of the essential problem, but parallels to it are hard to find. Certainly, however, a 'convulsion upon the nerves' would appear to have attacked the gentleman who managed Lord Lexington's estates, during the latter's diplomatic missions abroad. In 1695 he wrote as follows from Nottinghamshire: 'I wish I could persuade you to turn your plate into money, for if a Revolution should happen, and Mr. Mob is much dreaded, you may repent. I am sure the interest of your money will more than pay for fashion again.' He was presumably referring to the possibility of a political upheaval to be followed by an outbreak of mob violence, but I can find no trace of disturbance in Nottinghamshire in that year which might lend colour to the latter fear. The former was, as we shall see, always present in these years.[2]

Dr. Marshall gives some space in her book on *The English Poor in the Eighteenth Century* to a discussion of the indifference in this period to the possibility of social upheaval. For she holds this partly responsible for the increasing harshness of the social legislation of the period. She ascribes this indifference to the existence in this period, for the first time in English history, of a standing army.[3] To the place which can be assigned to the regular army in the maintenance of internal order some space must be devoted in our final chapter.[4] Its importance in this respect is clearly exaggerated by Dr. Marshall, and for an adequate explanation of the phenomenon with which she deals it is clearly necessary to go outside the purely administrative sphere.

[1] John Bellers, *Essays about the Poor, Manufactures, Trade, Plantations and Immorality and of the Excellence and Divinity of Inward Light*, 1699. Cf. Gooch, pp. 302–3; W. C. Braithwaite, *The Second Period of Quakerism*, 1919, chap. xx.

[2] *The Lexington Papers*, edited by the Hon. H. Manners Sutton, 1851, p. 87.

[3] D. Marshall, *The English Poor in the Eighteenth Century*, 1926, p. 8.

[4] See Chap. VII, *infra*.

If sporadic and ineffective rioting remained for the whole of this period and for three-quarters of the eighteenth century the sole form of working-class action, the reasons for this fact must be sought in the history of that class itself, in the changes in its status and morale. It is to be regretted that no attempt has yet been made to depict the social problems of this period as a whole, comparable with the work of Professor R. H. Tawney for an earlier period or that of J. L. and B. Hammond for a later one. The pioneer work of Mrs. M. D. George on London deserves to act as a stimulus for a series of studies of other areas. Failing these, one can only deal in brief with the more salient features in the history of certain sections of the working population.

One can, for instance, take the 'poor husbandmen' or small tenant farmers to whose plight Baxter refers. Since, according to Gregory King's estimate, they were responsible for one-eighth of the total population, their fortunes are of considerable importance. They were, except in areas where the proximity of a great city or of an industrial centre supplied them with a ready market, grievously hit by the fall in wheat-prices between the Restoration and the revolution.[1] The agricultural improvements of the age benefited not them but the larger landowners by whom they were being displaced. Professor Unwin traces here the source of an outflow from the land into industry which 'produces the new proletariat of textile workers which is to be found in the suburbs of London, in the clothing districts of the west and in south-east Lancashire in the first half of the eighteenth century'. With this proletariat we shall have to deal again, and the whole subject is still obscure. But there seems some reason for accepting Baxter's belief that the agricultural labourer, provided that he remained unmarried, was better off than the rack-rented 'poor husbandman'.[2]

The position of the wage-earner is likewise not readily ascertainable, nor in the country districts is it always clear to what extent his money wages represented his real income.

[1] See Appendix of Corn Prices.
[2] Professor G. Unwin's preface to the already cited treatise of Richard Baxter contains a summary of this question.

The view once held that in the reign of Charles II, at least, wages outran prices is now at best held to be non-proven.[1] Wage assessments were still issued. Most writers hold, however, that they were no longer actually enforced, and that the intervention of the justices was limited to the enforcement of contracts arrived at by private bargaining.[2] It seems clear that the assessments at any rate no longer followed the price of victuals, and that they must often have lagged behind the wages actually paid. It is thus impossible to determine the effect of short-term price-fluctuations upon wages.[3]

Taking the period as a whole, the general opinion would appear to be that agricultural wages did not keep pace with rising prices. Dr. Hampson holds, however, that the position of the single agricultural labourer was a very strong one throughout the latter half of the seventeenth century. 'There was', she writes, 'an actual scarcity of hands while at the same time the marked rise in the price of manufactured goods during the latter half of the seventeenth century, was not accompanied by a corresponding rise in the price of food products, a matter of prime significance in the rural labourer's cost of living.' The position of the unmarried labourer was helped, too, by the fact that the Act of Settlement was rarely applied against him.[4]

On the other hand, there can be no doubt at all of the miserable position of the married labourer. 'Although unemployment was not a widespread menace in rural

---

[1] G. N. Clark, *The Later Stuarts*, 1934, p. 38.

[2] Lipson, pp. 255–66; Heckscher, *Mercantilism*, English ed., 1935, i. 311–12; E. Hampson, *The Treatment of Poverty in Cambridgeshire*, 1934, pp. 51–7. S. A. Peyton maintains, on the other hand, in the introduction to the *Kesteven Quarter Sessions Records*, 1931, pp. cx–cxii, that the system was in operation throughout the Stuart period.

[3] See, for instance, the series of entries in the *Buckinghamshire County Records*, ed. le Hardy and Reckitt, 1933, i. 227–9, 386; ii. 44, 87, 125, 173, 204, 247, 288, 383, 422. In 1700 the justices were instructed to consider whether they should reissue the same assessments or whether change was needed. They confirmed the old rates. Ibid., pp. 248, 325. See also M. S. Gretton, *Oxfordshire Justices of the Peace*, 1934, p. lxiii; Gilboy, *Wages in Eighteenth Century England*, 1934, Introduction and p. 25; A. H. Hamilton, *Quarter Sessions from Queen Elizabeth to Queen Anne*, 1878; R. W. Kelsall, 'Two East Yorkshire Wage Assessments', *E.H.R.* lii; Chambers, pp. 283–4. Lipson's treatment of the question is inconclusive, ii. 386–95.

[4] Chambers, pp. 270–2 and 280; Hampson, p. 52.

Cambridgeshire at this date,' writes Dr. Hampson, 'statutory wages rarely met the needs of a large family. It was the unstable position of the married labourer which was the crux of the settlement problem.'[1] With this knowledge before them, it is not surprising that parish officers put every obstacle in the way of the movements of the married labourer. The laws of settlement were applied against him with almost as much rigour as they were against the aged, the infirm, children and women, and especially the members of the most inhumanly treated class of all, the unmarried mother or expectant mother. How, given what we know of their wages, this class managed to exist at all, neither contemporary nor modern writers seem able to explain.[2]

Furthermore, wherever enclosure progressed at the expense of cottagers and other very small holders, and of their rights of common, it had the effect of making them more and more dependent on wages alone. This must have affected their diet adversely, though it is noticeable that the wages themselves might be higher in enclosed villages where less labour was available.[3] Attempts were still made to prevent the evasion of the old laws forbidding the erection of cottages without four acres of land being attached. But this activity was dictated as much by a desire to avoid future calls on the parish for poor-relief as by any far-sighted idea of checking the growing landlessness of the agricultural labourer.[4]

To turn our attention from the agricultural to the industrial worker is to encounter a crop of difficulties not less formidable. The lack of transport facilities and local animosity against 'foreigners', together with the statutory restrictions on the movement of labour, caused considerable local variations in wage-rates.[5]

[1] Ibid., p. 126.
[2] D. Ogg, *England in the Reign of Charles II*, 1934, i. 85; W. G. Hoskins, *Industry, Trade and People in Exeter*, 1935, pp. 21–2. The latter notes that in Devonshire in the reign of William III more than one-fifth of the population were in receipt of poor-relief.
[3] G. Slater, *The English Peasantry and the Enclosure of the Common Fields*, 1907, chap. xi; Chambers, p. 284.
[4] *Hertford County Records*, ed. le Hardy, 1905, vii. 106 and 124. There are licences for such cottages in the Northamptonshire Sessions Records.
[5] Gilboy, *passim*.

Certain areas where there had been widespread dependence upon some particular form of economic activity, now in decline, were undeniably depressed. This was especially true, as we shall have cause to note, of the cloth-growing districts of the west of England. The hardships of the workers in this industry were intensified by the fact that the justices no longer enforced minimum wages.[1] The Cornish tin-mining districts also suffered heavily. Finally, on the Tyneside coalfield an ever increasing number of miners and transport workers depended upon an industry whose products could only be disposed of by coastal shipping. The interruptions in this coastal trade, caused by the naval wars, produced acute if temporary depressions which caused much misery.[2]

There seems otherwise little reason to believe that the artisan and industrial worker were failing to benefit by the marked general rise in the nation's prosperity. The position is further complicated by the fact that in years of comparative plenty the workers at this time were in the habit of seeking to benefit rather by working fewer days a week than by adding to their incomes. This at least suggests that wages had not yet been forced down to subsistence level and that they were, in fact, largely governed by tradition.[3]

Nevertheless, in the country as a whole there was a good deal of distress, and the various schemes for employing the poor in some form of self-supporting or even profitable colony or establishment were worked out against a menacing background of fact. But for most people the chief symptom of this flaw in the social system was the rise in the poor-rate. There, administration was the crux of the matter, but this, unaccompanied as it was by any clear thought on the economic causes of poverty and unemployment, was bound to be unsatisfactory so long as the parochial unit was adhered to. The old ideas of providing work broke down in spite of the attempts towards the end of our period to revive them in the new Union workhouses. Relief was on the whole probably

[1] R. H. Tawney, 'The Assessment of Wages in England by the Justices of the Peace', *Vierteljahrschrift für Sozial- und Wirtschaftgeschichte*, xi, 1913, and Chap. IV, *infra*.

[2] J. U. Nef, *The Rise of the British Coal Industry*, 1932, ii. 143–5.

[3] Lipson, iii. 266–7; Chambers, p. 277.

not ungenerous.[1] The chief hardship was, no doubt, that caused by the enforcement of the settlement laws. To the old fear of vagrancy was added the new one of rising rates. Even if we admit that the act of 1662 itself did nothing but regularize the common practice of parish officers, and that its administration by the justices was a humaner way of achieving the same ends, nothing can minimize the terrible hardships inflicted.[2] Even the view of Dr. Chambers, that the old whippings of vagrants died out in this period, is not borne out by the study of county records.[3] Furthermore, in the metropolitan district and other populous areas the act was applied in order to relieve local shopkeepers from the competition of pedlars, to which they attributed the decay of trade.[4]

To the problem of vagrancy and to its connexion with the problems of public order we shall return. Our immediate task is to see how the treatment of the poor illustrates one of the chief features in the social theory of the period. Even contemporaries were shortly to realize the moral implications of the settlement laws and to idealize by comparison the medieval treatment of the poor. Before the Reformation, wrote the author of a popular hand-book of administrative practice, there was no occasion for any such law as the Elizabethan poor-law; 'because such was the devotion of our Ancestors that there seemed to be a pious contention among them who should first bring their offering to a church'. 'We have now', he says elsewhere, 'Laws in force to confine

[1] Marshall, *passim*; S. and B. Webb, *The Old Poor Law, passim*.

[2] Stats. of Realm, 13 & 14 Car. II, cap. 12; Peyton, p. cv; Chambers, pp. 216–22; S. and B. Webb, op. cit., chap. vi.

[3] Chambers, p. 249; *North Riding Quarter Sessions Records*, vii. 135–6 and 191, n.; Northamptonshire Sessions Records.

[4] *C.S.P. Dom., 1675–6*, pp. 145, 399; *C.J.* ix. 328, 332, 335, 373; *Middlesex County Records*, iii. xlix–liii; E. Dowdell, *A Hundred Years of Quarter Sessions*, 1932, pp. 70–7; *Middlesex Sessions Records*, ed. le Hardy, 1905, p. xi; *Buckingham County Records*, ii. 91, 110, and *passim*; *Shropshire County Records*, i, 1901–2, p. 133. For a complaint from the inhabitants of Rochester that unless itinerant traders were suppressed they would be unable to pay scot and lot, rents, &c., see *C.S.P. Dom., 1691–2*, p. 34. Such traders could not be wholly dispensed with, and the fines shaded off into a licensing system as provided for in the statutes 8 & 9 Will. III, cap. 25, and 9 Will. III, cap. 27. Pedlars still played an essential if humble part in rural economy, supplying even important households with combs, laces, ribbons, &c. G. S. Thomson, *Life in a Noble Household*, 1937, p. 77.

men to certain places of Habitation, which is as a sort of imprisonment, not for a Fault, but for a misfortune in being poor, and it has been questioned by some, whether such Laws are fit to be introduced among us especially when so little care is taken to employ our Poor.'[1]

The poor-laws were characteristic of an age whose leading economic theorists held strongly to the doctrine that low wages were of great benefit to the nation. Proposals for the employment of the poor were considered from the point of view of the contribution which they might make to the lowering of costs in the export industries so that all might play their part in the great national game of beggaring the Dutch.[2]

The problem of unemployment was not the only one to meet with so dehumanized a response. Rarely indeed can national wealth as opposed to welfare have predominated to such an extent as it did in the minds of the ruling class of the period. Some historians even hold—we have quoted Dr. Feiling—that the economic drift of the century was towards a sharper demarcation of classes. 'In the main', writes Dr. Chambers, 'there were three social categories in the eighteenth century: the people of quality, the tradesmen and the poor. While the first two were divided from one another by recognized social distinctions, the third was divided from both by a social gulf.'[3] Conditions in the second half of the previous century were not dissimilar. The same phenomenon has even been detected in the towns, where one might have supposed that the tendencies of nascent capitalism towards social fluidity would already have made themselves felt.

That capitalism had or was to have the effect of giving, at least for a time, the possibility of rapid social advance to gifted individuals of the lower classes is undeniable. Many names could be quoted from this very period to illustrate the fact, exceptions which emphasized rather than concealed the rigidity of the social structure. And, whether or not it

[1] W. Nelson, *The Office and Authority of a Justice of the Peace*, 11th ed., 1736, pp. 79 and 50. E. M. Leonard, *The Early History of English Poor Relief*, and S. and B. Webb, *The Old Poor Law*, 1927, deal with this point.

[2] T. E. Gregory, 'The Economics of Employment in England, 1660–1713', *Economica*, vol. i, 1921.   [3] Chambers, p. 48.

was, in fact, disappearing, the assumption that this rigidity existed was fundamental in the social thought of the time. It was this which led economic pamphleteers to apply the word 'poor' not merely to those in receipt of relief but to the labouring-classes as a whole.[1]

Nor did the rise to wealth and power of selected individuals sweeten the lot of the less fortunate. In the country-side the relation of landlord and tenant was changing, as new men, whose social ethics, like their wealth, were the product of business or the law, replaced the older families who still cherished the tradition of paternalism.[2] In backward districts like Yorkshire, conservatives like Reresby might still keep open house at Christmas and maintain the now old-fashioned notion of hospitality. Occasionally even an eighteenth-century squire might put on patriarchal airs, and a good deal of open-handed, if carefully accounted for, charity was still practised by the great. But in most areas the old spirit was already dead.[3]

In a time of such marked social stratification, improvements in manners and morals percolated but slowly from the higher to the lower ranks of society. And the increasing civilization of even the upper classes in Restoration England must be held to have been largely superficial, if we take abstention from unnecessary violence to be the mark of a civilized man.

Largely for reasons of personal safety, all the members of the wealthier classes possessed arms and were trained in their use. Such as were needed for game and for self-defence against highwaymen and robbers might even be retained by political suspects when their arms were confiscated. Violent self-help in the face of a disputed lawsuit or will was not unknown and may explain many of the curt indictments for riot and trespass in quarter-sessions records.[4] In spite of the efforts of the government, it was a

[1] E. S. Furniss, *The Position of the Labourer in a System of Nationalism*, 1920, *passim*; Marshall, chap. i; R. H. Tawney, *Religion and the Rise of Capitalism*, 1926, pp. 264–5; Hampson, chap. v.

[2] H. E. Chesney, 'The Transference of Lands in England', *T.R.H.S.*, 1932, H. Phillips, *The Grandeur of the Law*, London, 1684; and Professor Tawney's (unpublished) Ford Lectures.

[3] Reresby, *Memoirs, passim*; Chambers, pp. 68–9; Thomson, pp. 225 and 361–4.

[4] For examples see P.C. 2. 73, pp. 455 and 503; 74, pp. 135 and 139; *C.S.P Dom.*, 1694–5, p. 443; *The Flemings in Oxford* (Oxford Hist. Soc.), 1. 159–60.

great age of duelling.[1] And finally, in times of political tension, assaults upon prominent partisans of either side became so common that in January 1671 it was remarked that 'the cutting of noses is grown use and fashion'.[2] The outrages of the so-called 'Mohocks' in 1712 were also probably due to political malice rather than to mere hooliganism.[3]

Nor was there anything in the attitude of the upper classes likely to predispose people to refrain from violence in matters of religion. The disorders which accompanied the efforts to enforce religious conformity under the various acts of the reign of Charles II belong to the general history of the reign and as such will fall to be mentioned in the next chapter. But a preacher personally unpopular or of suspect views, a clergyman wishing to enforce some order into the conduct of services in a way which conflicted with the established habits of his congregation, might then, as now, find his parishioners prepared to make violent demonstrations against him in the church itself, with no apparent regard for the sanctity of the place.[4]

In the sessions records of so disorderly an age there are naturally to be found innumerable cases of riot, riotous assault, and unlawful assembly whose direct cause cannot be known.[5] Cases of people being bound over to keep the peace, either generally or towards some specified person, also bulk largely in all such records.[6]

With brawling taking up so large a portion of the leisure of their betters, it is not surprising to find that the amusements of the lower classes were often of a violent nature.[7]

---

[1] Lapthorne shows no indignation at the frequency of duelling, regarding it as a venial fault compared with, for instance, sabbath-breaking. See also A. Bryant, *The England of Charles II*, 1934, pp. 116–18; *Verney Memoirs*, 1935, ii, chap. xlix.

[2] *H.M.C. Kenyon*, pp. 86–8.

[3] *The Wentworth Papers*, ed. J. Cartwright, 1883, pp. 277–8; Swift, *Correspondence*, ed. Ball, 1910–14, i. 323; *Journal to Stella*, ed. Temple Scott, pp. 351–62; Crawford, p. 533.

[4] *C.S.P. Dom.*, *1661–2*, p. 379; *1672–3*, p. 546; *P.C.R.* 79, p. 233; *Hertford County Records*, ii. 36–7, vii. 69; *Buckingham County Records*, ii. 387; *Surrey County Records*, vi. 127; *Middlesex County Records*, iii. 321.

[5] e.g. *Buckingham County Records*, ii. 62, 110, 118, 129, 138, 283, 309, 335, 347, 359, 387, 404.   [6] e.g. *Surrey County Records*, vi, *passim*.

[7] Sports which brought together large numbers of spectators were suspect, as they had been during the Commonwealth, as providing a cover for meetings of disaffected persons. In June 1696 there was a report that a number of suspects

Whether witch-hunting is to be classed as an amusement
may be questioned, but a witch-hunt certainly caused considerable rioting in July 1694, in villages on the Wiltshire-
Somerset border.[1] In 1710 the apparently harmless ancient
custom of rivalry between two Surrey villages for the possession of the annual maypole led to a riot in which two men
were killed.[2] The proclamations for properly observing the
sabbath and for the preventing of drunkenness and swear-
ing had thus a more than moral significance. Disorderly
alehouses and gatherings for games were always objects of
suspicion and often suppressed perhaps because of fears of
disorder.[3] Public rejoicings and public executions might
alike prove occasions for rioting. As might be expected,
theatres and fairs, too, contributed in London their quota
of disorder, so that the government had to intervene to
prevent unauthorized persons from obtaining admission.[4]

In September 1690 a clash took place at Bartholomew
Fair between the mob and some young noblemen who were
dancing in the cloisters of St. Bartholomew's hospital. The
latter, annoyed by the people pressing to be spectators of
their amusements, drew their swords, with the result that
nine people were seriously wounded.[5] In the following
year the lord mayor and aldermen accordingly ordered the
fair to be held for three days only instead of for a fortnight,
as previously.[6] This restriction does not appear to have
been of long duration, for in 1708 the Common Council
of the city decided that, the lease for Bartholomew Fair
expiring that year, 'for the future none should be kept for
stage-plays, raffling shops etc., which tend to debauchery;
but only three days for the sale of leather and cattle according

had resorted to a cock-fight at Sherborne. The Lords Justices ordered an inquiry
to be made as to the troops quartered in the district. *C.S.P. Dom., 1696*, p. 242.

1 *Wiltshire County Records*, 1932, pp. 279 ff.

2 *Wentworth Papers*, pp. 119–21.

3 For unlawful games at a place in the Strand see *Middlesex County Records*,
p. 181. For a description of a disorderly alehouse suppressed by the justice see
Hertford County Records, vii. 141. It was also considered that excessive indulgence
in pleasure was destroying the productive capacity of the working-classes. Furniss,
p. 152.

4 Luttrell, ii. 13; *C.S.P. Dom., 1665–6*, p. 92; *1673*, p. 420; *1673–5*, p. 231;
1689–90, p. 321.

5 Luttrell, ii. 99; *Portledge Papers*, p. 84.   6 Ibid., p. 118.

to its ancient custom'. A petition from the governors of the hospital, in favour of its being allowed to continue for fourteen days as before, was rejected.[1]

The May Fair in the parish of St. Martin's in the Fields was another frequent scene of disorder. In 1702 the high constable and several petty constables sent by the Westminster court to 'look for disorderly women and other lewd persons' were attacked by the mob and one of them killed.[2] In February 1708 the grand jury of Westminster presented May Fair as a nuisance to the city, and the lord chief justice promised to acquaint the queen with this in order to have all irregularities there suppressed.[3] In April, upon information of disorder there, the constables were instructed to attend to see that peace was maintained,[4] and in the following year the grand jury appears again to have addressed the queen, whereupon a proclamation was issued against the disorders.[5] Other lesser fairs were likewise proceeded against, and one at Hendon in 1697 was forbidden.[6]

All these things, however, while symptomatic enough of the moral condition of the people, were unimportant from the point of view of the administration. The really important social problems, which were closely related both to each other and to the question of public order, were those of vagrancy and of violent crime.

It would be platitudinous to insist upon the bad state of the roads at this period when the era of turnpikes was only just beginning.[7] Presentments for non-fulfilment of the statutory duties of road repair are especially characteristic of the records of outlying counties and of those responsible for the upkeep of the roads leading to London.[8] In one respect this may have helped to make easy the task of the administration in keeping order, since bad roads prevented

¹ Luttrell, vi. 311 and 322.

² *C.S.P. Dom.*, *Anne*, i. 83; ii. 63–6; *Middlesex County Records*, p. 241.

³ Luttrell, vi. 407.   ⁴ *Middlesex County Records*, p. 241.

⁵ Ibid. and Crawford, p. 530. Sir Nathaniel Curson, who held the letters patent for the fair, seems to have offered to surrender them. State Papers, Anne, 37 (no. 172 ?).

⁶ Dowdell, pp. 29–30; *Middlesex County Records*, p. 170.

⁷ Ernle, p. 282.

⁸ e.g. *North Riding Quarter Sessions Records* and the *Buckingham County Records*, *passim.*

the free and rapid movement of bodies of rioters about the country. On the other hand, it meant that a small band of rioters could easily terrorize the population of an almost isolated district. The provisions of the Act of Settlement, which were applied in order to relieve the rates against women, the young, and the infirm, were applied against the able-bodied largely from motives of fear.

In 1670, for instance, a band of marauders calling themselves Levellers successfully terrorized for some considerable period the country round Kempsey in Worcestershire, and attracted considerable attention.[1]

As we have seen, acts 'for the more effectual punishment of vagrants and sending them whither by law they ought to be sent' continued to be passed and to be put into effect throughout the period.[2] Evidence of local action in this respect is, as we have seen, readily available. At the Easter sessions of 1689 the Derbyshire quarter-sessions court was petitioned, by various inhabitants of the hundreds of High Peak and Scarsdale, to take further order with regard to the increased numbers of sturdy beggars who had grown insolent and threatening in the uncertainties of the times.[3] In Shropshire in 1691 the economic motive appears to have been uppermost, and it was ordered in the January sessions that 39 Eliz., cap. 4, against rogues and vagabonds be put into execution and that Scotchmen carrying packs be proceeded against as such.[4] Other local authorities also made strenuous efforts to check the depredations of vagrants, especially after the peaces of 1697 and 1713 had added to their numbers a multitude of disbanded soldiers. This they did by enforcing the vagrancy statutes, and especially by forbidding relief to all not possessed of legal passports showing that they had one of the recognized claims on charity.[5] The problem later became more one of finance than of

---

[1] *C.S.P. Dom.*, *1670*, pp. 597–8, and *1671*, pp. 18–19; *H.M.C. le Fleming*, p. 74; *V.C.H. Worcester*, iv. 456.

[2] Stats. of Realm, 11 Will. III, cap. 18; 1 Anne, cap. 13; 6 Anne, cap. 32; 13 Anne, cap. 26.

[3] J. C. Cox, *Three Centuries of Derbyshire Annals*, 1890, ii. 154.

[4] *Shropshire County Records*, i. 133.

[5] *Chester County Records, Sessions Book*, April 1697; *Buckingham County Records*, ii. 168 and 201; *North Riding Quarter Sessions Records*, vii. 135–6 and 234; Macaulay, vi. 399.

order, and quite early in the eighteenth century we find
beginning the practice of contracting with private individuals for the removal of vagrants, as in the case of other
local government services.[1] The system of recruitment for
the army and navy must have done much to remove the more
dangerous elements in the vagrant population.[2]

In 1706, however, there was a riot at Liverpool when the
municipal authorities tried to remove some squatters who
had been formally encouraged to settle in the castle grounds
by Lord Molyneux.[3]

Even more important, from the point of view of factors
making for disorder, was the enormous amount of violent
crime. In one area, the counties of the Scottish border, the
activities of the moss-troopers had long been a nuisance
to private property and public order alike. In 1662 the
magistrates of Northumberland and Cumberland were
authorized to levy a rate for the maintenance of bands of
armed men to deal with their activities, and parishes were
required to keep bloodhounds for the purpose of hunting
them down.[4] Successive statutes prolonged this enactment
throughout this period. Under the act of 18 & 19 Car. II,
cap. 3, it had been further enacted that benefit of clergy should
be taken away from this class of offenders, while under the act
of 19 & 20 Car. II, cap. 2, securities were to be taken from
those appointed in these areas to preserve law and order, to
compensate any one damaged through their default.[5]

In 1710 we have mention of the impossibility of serving
warrants among the border population, where the typical
crime of the period, coining (which had elsewhere suffered
a decline after the recoinage operations of 1695–6), was
still rife.[6] Riots due to attacks on customs officers will be
dealt with best in connexion with the opposition to the
government's taxation schemes, but here, too, the border
counties provided a fair share.[7]

Another area with specific problems of its own was Corn-

---

[1] Hamilton, pp. 267–8.   [2] See Chap. VI, *infra.*
[3] Sir J. Picton, *Records of Liverpool*, pp. 39–40.   [4] Macaulay, i. 298.
[5] See also Stats. of Realm, 1 Jac. II, cap. 14; 7 & 8 Will. III, cap. 17; 12 & 13
Will. III, cap. 6; 12 Anne, cap. 20.   [6] C.S.P. Dom., Anne, MS. pp. 572–7.
[7] See Chap. V, *infra.* For the participation of rival bands of smugglers in the
Carlisle election of 1705 see *H.M.C. Portland*, iv. 195.

wall, where there was on several occasions considerable trouble owing to the difference of opinion between the inhabitants and the government as to the rights of the former over the contents of ships cast upon their shores. Interference with their declared rights of indiscriminate plunder and the arrest of the plunderers was always likely to be followed by rioting on a large scale.[1]

Poaching was another crime which gave serious concern to the authorities, as it often led to mobs' breaking down park enclosures, a practice specially penalized under an act of 1696.[2] In 1700 a certain John Durham was appointed gamekeeper for Richmondshire and Northallertonshire, and the treasurer for the former area was ordered to pay him £5 as a yearly salary.[3] In 1689 there were many attacks upon game preserves under cover of the prevailing anti-popery cry.[4]

Largest in the public interest, however, loomed murder, burglary, and highway robbery.[5] Only the popular press of to-day provides in its unblushing interest in violent crime a parallel to the correspondence of Richard Lapthorne, who, in the intervals of reporting news of rare books for the west-country squire whose agent he was, delivered accounts of, and reflections upon, the latest crimes and executions.[6] A typical extract (from a letter of 1 November 1690) runs: 'The world with us is very unruly debauched and profane, aboundance of Robberies committed and vice very little checked by those in Authority which makes me feare God is yet providing greater scourge for the Nation which God

---

[1] G. R. Lewis, *The Stannaries*, 1908, p. 221; *C.S.P. Dom.*, *1698*, pp. 191–2; *1699*, pp. 77, 233, 258; W. E. H. Lecky, *History of England in the Eighteenth Century* (ed. of 1892), ii. 113–14. There was a riot over disputed rights to wreckage in Carmarthenshire in 1662. P.C. 2. 56, p. 339.

[2] Stats. of Realm, 9 Will. III, cap. 33. For game-preserving acts and their history see Sir William Holdsworth, *A History of English Law* (new. ed. 1922–7), iv. 503. Cf. Chambers, p. 75; Hamilton, p. 269.

[3] *North Riding Quarter Sessions Records*, vii. introduction.

[4] Crawford, p. 476; *C.S.P. Dom.*, *1689–90, passim.*

[5] Macaulay, i. 398. There seems no valid reason for the attribution of the rise of the professional highwayman to a period after the middle of the eighteenth century as is done by S. and B. Webb (*Statutory Authorities for Special Purposes*, p. 410). He was a ubiquitous figure in this period.

[6] 6,000 people witnessed the public execution of two women at Castledown, near Plymouth, in 1676. *C.S.P. Dom.*, *1676–7*, p. 54.

grant our humiliation and sincere repentance may divert.'[1] The abundance of crime went on throughout the period unchecked. Luttrell notes in February 1691 that there have been more robberies in London this winter than before within living memory.[2] And on 9 April 1692 Lapthorne writes: 'Murders have been committed almost every day this week last past.'[3]

This large criminal population, concentrated, as it was, around the capital, and containing in all probability the more desperate of the politically disaffected, was obviously a constant threat to order, and the administration was by no means so supine as Lapthorne would have us believe. Indeed, had it been possible by mere paper activity to deal with these problems, it would, no doubt, have been highly successful. The complete absence of a police force worthy of the name made effective action almost impossible. A justice of the king's bench was at one period entrusted with the task of suppressing highwaymen. But this had no greater permanent result than the production of a prematurely optimistic report.[4] At other times attempts were made to stimulate local justices to activity by means of proclamations.[5] The statute of 1692, which offered rewards for the discovery and apprehension of highway robbers, did little more than encourage the trade of informer which so flourished at this time, to the despair of successive secretaries of state.[6] In February 1694 a suggestion was made in parliament that there should be 'a middle punishment for highwaymen betwixt hanging and acquitting viz: exposed to labour and that workhouses be set up for that purpose and for employing beggars and poor people'.[7] This is interesting as showing that some contemporaries at

---

[1] *Portledge Papers*, p. 90. Pamphlets containing accounts of the latest crimes were purchased for the Earl of Bedford as well as others on demonology and witchcraft. Thomson, p. 274.   [2] Luttrell, ii. 170.

[3] *Portledge Papers*, p. 135. In November 1692 nine butchers on their way to Thame were held up by nine highwaymen, who, having robbed them, made them sit in a row and drink King James's health, and then told them to sue the hundred for this money. *C.S.P. Dom., 1691–2*, p. 500.

[4] *C.S.P. Dom., 1671–2*, p. 298.

[5] e.g. Crawford, pp. 412, 486, 491.

[6] Stats. of Realm, 4 Will. & Mar., cap. 8. See Chap. VII, *infra*.

[7] *Portledge Papers*, p. 170.

least realized the connexion of the amount of crime with an over-harsh criminal law and with pauperism.

There is no information as to the success of a mechanical burglar-alarm patented in the same month by an enterprising merchant eager to catch a rising market.[1] But an act of 1698 for the better apprehending of those guilty of burglary and similar crimes mentions that such crimes 'are of late years much increased'.[2] More progressive in spirit was an act of the next reign which repealed a clause in the former one making burning in the cheek a part of the punishment for such crimes. This, it was found, rendered the offenders' future employment impossible and forced them to remain professional criminals.[3]

In considering this evidence of the prevalence of violence, it is essential to realize the amount of cruelty and brutality common in the everyday life of the period. Every one whipped those over whom he had authority, and the frequent assaults, for instance, by masters on their apprentices were only occasionally punished.[4]

If order in the face of this was on the whole maintained, it was due to no abstract respect for the officials whose duty it was to preserve the peace. At no time, perhaps, has it been more true that the policeman's lot is not a happy one. The constable's unpaid duties often involved considerable danger.[5] Assaults upon constables and watchmen in the performance of their duties were no less frequent than those we shall have cause to note made upon tax-collectors, customs officers, and excisemen.[6] The arrest of a suspect might always be followed by his rescue at the hands of his neighbours.[7] In London, in 1694, an attempt by five bailiffs to arrest a gentleman led to the drawing of swords and to the death of the gentleman and of two of the bailiffs.[8] Even the county gaols were not immune from attacks by riotous

---

[1] C.S.P. Dom., 1694–5, p. 17.

[2] Stats. of Realm, 10 Will. III, cap. 12.

[3] Ibid., 6 Anne, cap. 9.

[4] J. C. Jeaffreson in the introduction to vol. iii of the Middlesex County Records, pp. xxxix–xl.   [5] Bryant, pp. 180–1.

[6] e.g. Middlesex County Records, iii. 362.

[7] e.g. Surrey County Records, vi. 128; Hertford County Records, ii. 38–9; vii. 87; Cheshire County Records, passim; and Chap. VII, infra.

[8] C.S.P. Dom., 1695, p. 285.

mobs bent on the rescue of prisoners, as happened, for instance, in Stafford in 1690.[1] There was excellent reason for the large number of new gaols built in this period.[2]

The main reason for the comparative peace of the country was the scattered nature of the population.[3] Where it was concentrated, even in small manufacturing or market towns or in seaports, it was likely to be turbulent enough.

The exception is the capital itself. The enormous growth of London is perhaps the most important single feature of the social history of the period. It was accompanied, too, by a process of occupational and social differentiation among its internal divisions—a process accelerated by the Great Fire. This helped to magnify the problems confronting its chaotic array of local authorities. Their failure to deal with them is sufficient explanation of the horror with which, more than a century before the time of Cobbett, this morbid phenomenon, as it seemed, was universally regarded. Vain attempts were made to revive the early Stuart policy of checking the growth of the metropolis by legislation or by penal taxation on new buildings.[4] In 1718 there was a proposal to tax bricks and tiles with this same end in view.[5]

John Bellers, in recommending to the public his projected 'colleges of industry', wrote that they would 'prevent the loss of Thousands of People, that by going to London drop there now, as untimely fruit, this City being one tenth of the People of England, it is too numerous in proportion to the rest of the Kingdom; for what it hath more than its proportion, they must live either by sharping or begging or starve'.[6]

This mass of people of the poorest classes, whose miserable condition at a slightly later period has been so power-

---

[1] C.S.P. Dom., 1689–90, p. 459.

[2] Many sets of county records mention rates for the construction or reconstruction of prisons.

[3] Chambers comments on the absence of organized crime in eighteenth-century Nottinghamshire compared with the 'systematic lawlessness which made everyday life in London streets a perpetual adventure'. Op. cit., p. 69.

[4] Reresby Memoirs (ed. Browning, 1937), p. 376; Webb, Statutory Authorities for Special Purposes, p. 399. See also N. Brett-James, The Growth of Stuart London, 1936, and the chapter by O. H. K. Spate in An Historical Geography of England, ed. by H. C. Darby, 1936.

[5] E. R. A. Seligman, The Shifting and Incidence of Taxation, 1899, pp. 24–5.

[6] Bellers, p. 5.

fully described by Mrs. M. D. George, was already a serious problem, and one which had outgrown the old arrangements for relief in which public assistance was expected to act as merely supplementary to private charity.[1] Besides the fluctuations of prosperity incidental to an industrial population, that of London suffered in other ways from economic instability. Much incidental employment was given by the great households when the nobility and gentry were keeping state in town, and their absence for any reason brought much distress.[2] The food supply and the fuel supply depended, the latter wholly, the former in part, upon an easily interrupted coastal trade. We cannot do more than indicate here the efforts at intervention occasionally made by the government, though the subject well deserves study.[3] But it is worth noting that, to the ministers of William III, at least, an effective method of dealing with distress was to direct the bishop of London to have house-to-house collections made for the relief of the poor.[4]

Such being the case, it is not to be wondered at that the London mob was always ready to swell any disturbance, whether or not its own interests were directly affected. Apart from its intervention in the strife of parties, which we shall have occasion to discuss later, the London mob could always be relied on to manifest its patriotism by rioting against the ambassador of the power least in favour. Thus it took sides with the Spaniards against the French in the famous quarrel over precedence in September 1661, demonstrated against the Dutch ambassador in March 1665 and in November 1668, and again against the Spanish ambassador in September 1686, when anti-popery feelings were growing. In February 1710 a demonstration against the Portuguese ambassador was expected.[5]

[1] For these see the already cited work of E. M. Leonard.

[2] For an example of this see the work of G. S. Thomson, already cited. In December 1662 the churchwardens of St. Margaret's, Westminster, petitioned the king to continue his benevolence of £100, paid in the previous year, since many of those who used to relieve the poor were out of town.

[3] For measures to deal with the coal-shortage in London during the second Dutch war see C.S.P. Dom., 1664–5, passim; C.S.P. Ven., 1664–6, p. 92.

[4] C.S.P. Dom., 1693, p. 424; 1696, p. 447; 1698, p. 26.

[5] Ibid., 1661–2, pp. 100–5; C.S.P. Ven., 1664–6, p. 85; 1666–8, p. 321; H.M.C. Portland, iii. 397; Wentworth Papers, p. 109.

The majority of the London disturbances did not, however, come from the labouring population as a whole, but from one particular class—the notorious apprentices. It was not merely in London that their privileged holidays, notably Shrove Tuesday, often led to riots. We have records of several such disturbances, often directed against houses of ill fame, in provincial towns in these years. Worcester and Bristol were notable scenes of such rioting.[1] In London the very numbers of the apprentices made them and the disorders they created far more formidable. It was calculated that there were three or four apprentices to one master, and that if they got out of hand the train-bands would be insufficient to put them down.[2] This foreboding was to prove accurate.

It was partly a sense of corporate loyalty that made them formidable. In March 1664 two apprentices were sentenced to the pillory and imprisoned for beating their master, and it was only after two days of rioting that the militia were able to restore order.[3] The execution of an apprentice in June 1695 was considered certain to lead to a riot.[4]

Most serious of all these disturbances were those of March 1668, when the original design of pulling down the houses of ill fame led to the opening of the prisons and to several days of disorder which necessitated the calling-out of the horse guards and other troops before quiet was finally restored.[5] It cannot be doubted that what worried the authorities on this occasion was the rumour—one not apparently without foundation—that political discontent was at the bottom of the whole affair. Old soldiers of Oliver's, the bugbears of this generation of administrators, as were the Jacobites of the next, were supposed to have fomented the trouble. Such a pamphlet as the mock *Whores Petition* (to Lady Castlemaine), together with remarks overheard from the rioters themselves, suggested that the court at Whitehall might easily commend itself to their puritanical zeal as a

[1] *C.S.P. Dom., 1667*, p. 560; J. Latimer, *Annals of Bristol in the Seventeenth Century*, 1900, p. 353.   [2] Ibid., *1667–8*, p. 310.

[3] *C.S.P. Ven., 1664–6*, p. 10.   [4] *C.S.P. Dom., 1694–5*, p. 489.

[5] Ibid., *1667–8*, pp. 306–24; *Middlesex County Records*, iii. xiii–xvii, 8–12; *Pepys's Diary*, March 24 and 25; P.C. 2. 60, p. 237; *State Trials*, ii. 583–90; and Chap. VII, *infra*.

worthy object for destruction.[1] In the same year rumours spread that there was a design to fire the rest of the city on May Day, and the apprentices were forbidden to go out on that day.[2]

In April 1670 there was again talk of a rising of the apprentices, who were said to claim that English trade was being ruined by excessive imports, especially from France. Excitement was aroused by political rumours, the most notable story circulating being that of an alliance between France and the Turks for the invasion of England.[3] Political discontent led to further tumults in 1680, and the leader of the apprentices admitted to a design to pull down the houses of ill fame and conventicles.[4] Further rioting among them took place in September 1682.[5]

Some at least of these outbursts were due to the precarious economic position of the apprentices rather than to mere youthful high spirits. The position in particular trades will concern us later. It is sufficient to note here the general relaxation of the old laws governing apprenticeship which was so marked a feature of the economic life of the post-civil war period. This led to the over-crowding of certain industries, at least, with young workers, taken on nominally as apprentices but in reality to provide cheap labour, with no guarantee of steady employment when their years of apprenticeship were over. And in the face of the growing demand for a free labour market the legislature, while it could not but notice these abuses, soon ceased to have the will or the power to deal with them.[6] A mass of inflammable material thus existed in the heart of the metropolis itself, ready fuel for the malice of the political agitator and a constant source of worry to harassed statesmen.

The actual criminal population of the country not unnaturally found its centre where so much of the nation's

---

[1] The government failed in their attempt to prosecute the publisher of this pamphlet, as so often in their proceedings against seditious libels. *C.S.P. Dom.*, *1667–8*, pp. 306, 354–65, 378, 510, 519, and Chap. II, *infra*.

[2] *H.M.C. le Fleming*, p. 56.

[3] *C.S.P. Dom.*, *1670*, pp. 146–7, 175–7.

[4] Ibid., *1689–90*, pp. 422–4.

[5] *Hatton Correspondence*, ii. 18.

[6] Lipson, iii. 286–92.

movable wealth was gathered.[1] It is unnecessary to repeat
Macaulay's famous description of the collection of wrong-
doers of all kinds gathered in the shelter of the immunity of
Whitefriars.[2] A riot in July 1691 between them and the
gentlemen of the Temple resulted in an attack upon the
sheriff with the loss of two or three lives, and in the calling-
out of the foot guards before the disturbances were finally
quelled.[3] The immunity of the Savoy was also a source of
trouble.[4] The mint at Southwark was yet another place
where criminals could band themselves together to resist the
forces of the law. The privileges of Whitefriars and the
Savoy were annulled in 1697, those of the Southwark mint
not until 1723, in spite of a petition of the commons in
1706.[5]

Only Oxford rivalled London in turbulence, for the
undergraduates of the day far outshone their successors in
the scope of their nocturnal disorders.[6]

In the capital there was always a certain amount of sullen
hostility towards members of the upper classes. Reresby
noted this phenomenon as a new one when he wrote an
account of his visit there during the Interregnum. 'The
citizens and common people of London had then so far
imbibed the customs and manners of a commonwealth', he
wrote, 'that they could scarce endure the sight of a gentleman, so that the common salutation to a man well-dressed
was French Dog or the like.' In the Restoration period
any one incurring the animosity of the crowd was likely to
be mobbed.[7] On days of public rejoicing the streets were
quite impassable, and the bad reputation of the London mob
was accepted as a matter of course, and continued into the
following century.[8]

One final terror of the London streets had nothing to do

[1] S. and B. Webb, *Statutory Authorities*, p. 408. There was a great increase in
crime in London after the Great Fire. *C.S.P. Dom.*, *1666–7*, pp. xi–xii.

[2] Macaulay, i. 380.

[3] Luttrell, iii. 86; *Portledge Papers*, p. 113.

[4] *C.S.P. Dom.*, *1679–80*, p. 352.

[5] *C.J.* xv. 147, 169–70; Lecky, *History of England*, ed. of 1892, ii. 109–10.

[6] *C.S.P. Dom.*, *1678*, pp. 183–4; A. Wood, *Life and Times*, ed. Clark, 1891, iii.
42–3, 130, 178, 246, 304, 307.

[7] *Reresby Memoirs*, pp. 21–2 and 403; Luttrell, iv. 451.

[8] *Wentworth Papers*, pp. 154–5.

with the 'mob'. The younger members of the nobility, not content with insisting, in spite of governmental prohibition, on settling their own disputes with the sword, indulged in the nocturnal habit of assaulting in the streets harmless passers-by and, even more frequently, the officers of the watch. The records of the period are full of such affrays.[1]

London, indeed, seems to have been a city where the very children were capable of causing a riot.

'One cow-keeper nigh this city', wrote the Reverend Robert Kirk in the diary of his London visit, 'hounded his dog at a city boy washing in one of his cow-ponds which so hurt him that in a few days he died. He was no sooner buried than there came thousands of boys and killed most of the man's cows, threw down his house to the ground, encamped several days, and could not be pacified by the train-bands pluffing powder at them nor by the Mayor or my Lord Craven till the cow-keeper was delivered into their hands whom they led to prison and he was banished the kingdom for fourteen years.'[2]

Such was the social background of the economic experiments, the dynastic and party strife, and the critical wars of the period. Such were the problems with which an undeveloped administrative system was called upon to deal in a country where administrative action was for ever held in check by the universal respect for the rights of the individual—rights jealously upheld by a legal system of greater antiquity and of more moral authority than any department of state.

The task of maintaining order was not easy, and rarely indeed was any area of the country for long in as pleasant a state as was the hundred of Ramsbury in Wiltshire when its jury made the following presentment to the October sessions of 1691:

'Upon our oathe we have no information to present anything presentable neither do we to the best of our knowledge know of anything to present in the hundred of Ramsbury for and in behalf of their Majesties King William and Queen Mary whom God grant long to reign which is and shall be the prayer of us whose names are hereunder subscribed.'[3]

[1] H.M.C. le Fleming, p. 76; Luttrell, ii. 234 and 238; Portledge Papers, p. 110; Hatton Correspondence, vol. i, passim.
[2] London and Middlesex Archaeological Society Transactions, vii, 1936, p. 134. The date of this incident was July 1687. H.M.C. Downshire, i. 255–6.
[3] Wiltshire County Records, p. 276.

II

THE POLITICAL BACKGROUND

'THE fact that Charles died peaceably in his royal bed', writes the most recent historian of his reign, 'has led posterity to underestimate the elements of precipitancy and anxiety from which no statesman of his reign could altogether escape.'[1] To treat of the popular disorders of the period and to ignore this fact would be to distort the picture. But the occasional disorders which arose out of the political and religious conflicts of the time are not particularly illuminating. They throw little additional light on what we already know of the predominant passions of these troubled generations. The outbreaks of disorder reflect the upheavals through which the country had passed and show how deeply implanted was the fear of yet further turmoil. We have noted how prone to violence was the mass of the population, and must remember how easily that population was stirred by agitation or even by mere rumour. 'The country is as it ever was and ever will be,' wrote the earl of Peterborough in February 1664, 'composed of brutes who do nothing but as instigated by others more industrious, interested and cunning.'[2]

In the political sphere again it was the London mob that was deemed most dangerous, and although it is not until the Sacheverell riots in Anne's reign that its intervention in politics came to a head, the fear of it was ever present.

The years immediately after 1660 were marked by the rapid disillusionment of those of Charles's subjects who had hoped that the Restoration would usher in a new era of toleration and national reconciliation.[3] The malcontents in London, fifth-monarchy men, quakers, and other sectaries, were rendered formidable by the presence among them of numerous Cromwellian soldiers whose careers had been

[1] Ogg, i. 210. The whole of this work has been invaluable in writing the present chapter. The chief primary source has been the *Calendar of State Papers, Domestic Series.*

[2] *C.S.P. Dom., 1663–4,* p. 496.

[3] For the first five years of the reign, the *Calendar of State Papers, Venetian Series,* has proved useful.

abruptly terminated by the return of the king. Venner's
rising in January 1661, while in itself insignificant, revealed
on how slender a basis of consent the restored monarchy
in fact rested.[1] Nor was this the last occasion when discontent manifested itself in overt disturbance. During
the temporary absence of the king and court on 29 April
the sectaries seized upon the occasion of indulging in a
riot.[2]

Disaffection was by no means confined to London. From
all over the country came reports of gatherings hostile to the
régime. The most harmless of religious meetings on the
part of the dissenters was sufficient to cause alarm. For this
constant state of panic the unpreparedness of the administration was in large part responsible. Financial stringency,
and the parliament's not ill-grounded dislike of a regular
army, prevented Charles from retaining more than a small
number of trained troops. Parliamentary delays and local
difficulties prevented the trained bands and militia from
reaching a condition of effectiveness for some considerable
time.[3] The slighting of the city walls of places where dissenters were supposed to be numerous showed how anxious
the government was lest a local rising might maintain itself
for long enough to develop into a national movement.[4]

In 1662 the general scarcity of money, enhanced by the
new taxation and the prevailing high price of food, swelled
the general discontent. In the politico-ecclesiastical sphere
the Act of Uniformity closed the doors to hopes of comprehension and reconciliation. The first overt disturbances took
place in the provinces when the nonconforming ministers
were ejected on St. Bartholomew's day.[5] The sale of Dun-
kirk lowered the government's prestige, and it was feared
that the disbanded soldiers from its garrison would be
dangerous.[6] In November and December there was talk
first of a rising in London and then of a plot to assassinate
Charles. The name of Ludlow, most feared of the surviving

---

[1] Ranke, *History of England*, English ed. 1875, iii. 356–9.
[2] *C.S.P. Ven.*, *1659–61*, p. 284.
[3] The two terms are not always distinguished, but 'trained bands' or 'train-bands'
usually refers to the militia of the towns. See Chap. VII, *infra*.
[4] *C.S.P. Dom.*, *1661–2*, pp. 423–4; *C.S.P. Ven.*, *1661–4*, pp. 161, 169, 180.
[5] Ibid., p. 185.   [6] Ibid., pp. 204–5.

republicans, makes an ominous appearance among the reports of government agents.[1]

Thenceforward reports of plots come in thick and fast, chiefly from the western and northern counties. There was even talk of Spanish aid for a projected rising.[2] This agitation culminated in the so-called Derwentdale plot in 1663. It was frustrated only by the vigilance of the authorities in the north and by the completeness of their preparations.[3] Minor outbreaks at York, Lancaster, Nottingham, and Chichester showed that no part of the country could be regarded as wholly reliable and at peace.[4]

The frustration of the northern plot did not end the activity of the discontented. 1664 was another year troubled with rumour. The war with the Dutch, now obviously approaching, was thought by some to be likely to give the disaffected their opportunity.[5] Others argued that the war was a diversion intended by the court to keep the people quiet.[6] If that was so, their wishes were, in part at least, to be gratified.

But before the attention of the nation was diverted to the struggle with its great commercial rival further measures were passed in the ecclesiastical sphere which were to have profound political and social effects. For the Conventicle Act and the Five Mile Act, if they did nothing to stamp out dissent, did establish in the country a class which had apparently nothing to hope for from the existing régime and which was therefore constantly suspected of wishing to overthrow it.

'In a sense,' writes Mr. Ogg, 'the so-called Clarendon Code was really panic legislation, due not so much to zeal on behalf of Anglican doctrine or discipline, as to a form of national hysteria which did not find its full expression until the Popish Plot. These acts were passed when the air was heavy with rumours of rebellions and insurrections; it needed only a few authentic plots to justify such fears in the minds of the legislature.'[7]

---

1 *C.S.P. Dom.*, *1661–2*, pp. 568 and 593, and *passim*.

2 Ibid., *1663–4*, pp. 129–30.

3 H. Gee, 'The Derwentdale Plot', *T.R.H.S.* 3rd ser., xi, 1917.

4 *C.S.P. Ven.*, *1661–4*, p. 267.

5 *C.S.P. Dom.*, *1663–4*, p. 566.

6 Ogg, loc. cit.   7 Ibid., p. 208.

During the period of the war itself we find much talk of disaffection but little sign of real danger. The plague year, 1665, was also a year of great economic distress, and the weight of taxation upon a poverty-stricken population still formed a theme for opponents of the régime. In the north, too, where complaints were loudest, the malcontents were encouraged, not for the last time, by the news of serious disaffection in Scotland. The militia were, however, now in better shape, and order was maintained. Apart from a riot directed against Clarendon in January 1666,[1] even the London mob was comparatively peaceful, though there was much anxiety lest the Great Fire be succeeded by disturbances.[2] This is noteworthy, as it marks the beginning of the period when all untoward accidents were ascribed to the machinations of the 'papists', thus foreshadowing the outburst of national hysteria at the time of the Popish Plot.

Considered in the light of the statistical evidence, it is indeed remarkable how deeply ingrained was the fear of 'popery'. A document among the State Papers for 1693 gives the number of catholic freeholders as 13,856, as against 108,676 dissenters and 2,477,254 adherents of the Establishment. The same document gives 4,940 as the number of 'papists' fit to bear arms.[3] The only area where they were sufficiently numerous to be taken into account as a political factor was the north-west, where, in the years 1680–2, we find rioting against attempts to enforce the recusancy laws in Lancashire.[4]

The years immediately after the conclusion of peace were also comparatively peaceful. The apprentices' riot in London in 1668 and an occasional outburst, such as that among 'the meaner sort' in Taunton in May of that year, during the celebration of a royalist defeat in the Civil War, showed that the cry of 'liberty of conscience' could still be powerful.[5] The continual reports of activity on the part of the dissenters and of the remissness of local authorities with regard to this

---

[1] *C.S.P. Ven.*, *1664–6*, p. 244.

[2] C. J. Hartmann, *Clifford of the Cabal*, 1937, p. 119.

[3] *C.S.P. Dom.*, *1693*, p. 445.

[4] P.C. 2. 69, pp. 113, 122, 126, 469; *C.S.P. Dom.*, *1680–1*, pp. 32, 49, 51–2; *H.M.C. Kenyon*, pp. 132–5.

[5] *Supra*, p. 30; *H.M.C. le Fleming*, p. 56.

led, however, to a new outburst of persecuting zeal. By the act of 1670, 22 Car. II, cap. 4, 'persons permitting conventicles to be held in their houses were to be fined £20, and constables were authorized to break into enclosed premises in search of conventicles. This Act was followed (May 1670–April 1671) by an intensive campaign against the sects, when the militia was called upon to disperse conventicles and offenders were dealt with summarily at Quarter Sessions.'[1] This not unnaturally led to a good deal of disorder both in London and in provincial towns such as Hull and Bristol, where there were large communities of nonconformists. The militia and the trained bands were constantly requisitioned to prevent or put down minor disturbances, and there was much talk of insurrection.

Neither the war nor the Declaration of Indulgence gave the government immediate respite, and the agitation was fanned by seditious literature largely of Dutch provenance. But as the foreign policy of Charles became more and more equivocal the attention of the nation was once more diverted from the prosecution of dissent. The years of Danby's ascendancy, though scarcely a few months passed without the rumour of a plot, were the quietest of the reign.

These years were, however, marked beneath the surface by the growth of anti-French and anti-catholic feeling, and of suspicion of the designs of a monarch now endowed with a considerable force of regular troops not needed for overseas service. By 1678, 'Charles, it is true, had not succeeded in obtaining the French money, but he kept his army, the gift of a House of Commons which had come to be in terror of the weapon it had placed in his hands. All the fears and hatreds steadily accumulating for a decade were now to be unloosed in a wild panic, and a fierce storm preceded the calm for which Charles yearned.'[2]

It would be useless to describe here either the course of political events in the next few years or their contribution to the sum of popular disorders in the period.[3] There were severe riots during the elections to the exclusion parlia-

---

[1] Ogg, i. 207. For the persecution of the quakers, who suffered most by this, see Braithwaite, *passim*.   [2] Ogg, ii. 558.

[3] There is a wholly admirable account in Ogg, chaps. xvi and xvii.

ments. After the crisis had been surmounted further riots marked the renewal of the persecution of the dissenters. Finally there were the disturbances which accompanied Monmouth's progress through the country in 1682. But all those are interesting chiefly for the evidence they afford of organization behind them. Further study may well elucidate more about the technique of agitation in this formative period of party history, but enough is known to show how far advanced was the knowledge of the means by which popular restlessness might be turned into party channels.[1]

It was not only parliamentary elections which provided urban mobs with a chance to take a violent part in politics. For previous riots on the occasion of municipal elections the practice of indiscriminate 'treating' was no doubt in part to blame.[2] There had, for instance, been a riot in Liverpool over the mayoral election of 1673.[3] The growing definiteness of party divisions and the attack upon the corporation charters now embittered municipal divisions, and henceforward we have a series of riots marking the vicissitudes of municipal politics. Nottingham was particularly disturbed with riots in 1678, 1682, and 1684.[4] But it did not stand alone.

The 'calm for which Charles yearned' was never, in fact, to come in his reign, nor in that of his successor. After examining the cross-currents of agitation and the disorders of the last years of the reign, Monmouth's rising is seen as the almost inevitable culmination of their turbulence. 'The real interest of the rebellion', writes Professor Clark, 'is neither military nor picturesque but social. It was the last popular rising in the old England.'[5] But although the depressions in the mining industry of the Mendips and in

---

[1] There are some interesting descriptions of all this in *H.M.C. Ormonde*, new series, iv.

[2] *Records of the Borough of Nottingham*, v. 379.

[3] Picton, *Records of Liverpool*, i. 246–7.

[4] P.C. 2. 66, p. 492; 67, pp. 67–8 and 75; *C.S.P. Dom.*, *1682*, p. 437; *Catalogue of James Ward's Library of Books relating to Nottinghamshire*, p. 16. Riots over municipal elections were not confined to the reign of Charles. There were disturbances at Dunwich in 1696 and 1698, and at Devizes in 1707. P.C. 2. 76, pp. 392 and 420; 77, pp. 267–9; *C.S.P. Dom.*, Anne, MS. pp. 443 and 465.

[5] Clark, pp. 114–15.

the woollen industry of Somerset help to explain the ease
with which Monmouth drew recruits from among the working-classes, it is possible to exaggerate this aspect of the
matter. There seems no evidence of economic or social aims
on the part of his adherents, and his choice of the area as
one in which to raise the signal of revolt was dictated not by
the prevalence of distress but by its noted protestantism.

Religious prejudice working upon the mob seems to have
been the true source of trouble in this period. In the summer
of 1686 there were anti-catholic riots at Bristol, and in
London the trained bands had to struggle hard to put down
the anti-catholic manifestations of the apprentices.[1] In the
critical autumn of 1688, the growing tension in the capital
was marked by another succession of outbursts directed
against the catholics.[2]

It has always been held as a testimony to the political
good sense of Englishmen that the great Revolution of 1688,
with its far-reaching political and constitutional consequences, should have been carried through without bloodshed. To contemporaries, the simplicity and ease of the
operation were less apparent, and there were those who felt
in the days following the flight of James II that the foundations of society itself were threatened by the violence of
members of social strata which had long appeared sub-
merged. It is true that the actual mobilization of the mass of
the country gentry in favour of the prince of Orange was
on the whole carried out without serious disorder. The
exceptions were the north-western counties, where the
survival of a large number of adherents of the catholic faith
served to add emphasis to the protestantism of their neighbours. In Cheshire an attack by the Molyneux faction upon
Lord Delamere's house was only averted by the flocking to
that magnate's banner of considerable forces among whom
personal, almost feudal, considerations seem to have played
a more prominent part than political or religious zeal.[3] The

---

[1] Latimer, p. 439; *Verney Memoirs*, 1899, ii. 447.

[2] *H.M.C. le Fleming*, p. 214; *Hatton Correspondence*, ii. 95; R. Sharpe, *London and
the Kingdom*, 1894, ii. 533; *The Autobiography of Sir John Bramston*, 1845, pp. 332
and 339–40.

[3] *H.M.C. le Fleming*, p. 225; Cheshire County Records, Sessions Rolls for
1690. The same strong protestant feeling had led to rioting in Cheshire during

progress of the Lancashire and Cheshire contingents into the neighbouring counties appears also to have caused a certain amount of worry there as to the possibility of maintaining order.[1]

Meanwhile, elsewhere in the country, isolated incidents revealed the growing impatience of the people. On 27 November it was reported that thirty of the king's troops had been killed in a clash with the populace at Uxbridge.[2] At the beginning of December there were attacks upon catholic priests by the Cambridge mob, and vestments and other articles of the catholic ritual were destroyed at Sidney Sussex College.[3] In Newcastle a 'mass-house' was sacked and used by 'Jack Pudding and his brethren for a Play-House'.[4] On 1 December there were attacks upon the houses of Bristol 'papists'.[5]

It was not, however, until the flight of James gave the signal for the unleashing of popular hatred, and his order to disband his forces its apparent opportunity, that mob violence became serious. The night of 11 December saw in London the sacking and burning by the mob of catholic chapels and of the houses of several foreign ministers.[6] The meeting next day of the Lords under Halifax's chairmanship, and their declaration threatening such action with prompt punishment and ordering all protestant officials to continue to exercise their functions and, if necessary, to call out the militia, were insufficient at once to put an end to the disorder.[7] On 13 December the Lords further ordered that the trained bands of the Tower Hamlets should, if necessary, fire on the mob, and placed the horse and foot guards, as well as some cannon, at various strategic points in Westminster.[8] This

---

Monmouth's rebellion. Lord Delamere was on that occasion tried for treason on very unsatisfactory evidence and acquitted. See Ormerod's *History of Cheshire*. For a general account of the Revolution see H. C. Foxcroft, *Life of Halifax*, 1893, ii, chap. ix.　　　　　　　　　　　　　　[1] *H.M.C. Cowper*, ii. 344–5.
[2] *Hatton Correspondence*, ii. 114–15.　　[3] *H.M.C. le Fleming*, p. 226.
[4] Great News from Nottingham, Bodley, fol. θ, 590 (43).
[5] Latimer, p. 451.
[6] *Reresby Memoirs*, p. 537; *Verney Memoirs*, ii. 467–8.
[7] Crawford, i. 473.
[8] Foxcroft, ii. 34–5. For the prompt action of the Lords, which probably saved the city from even more serious outbreaks, see Turberville, *House of Lords in the Reign of William III*, 1913, chap. vi.

was sufficient to stop any more serious disturbances, but there was some difficulty in safeguarding the lives of several particularly obnoxious persons, notably that of Lord Chancellor Jeffreys, whom the mob 'threatened to dissect'.[1] Attacks on 'mass-houses' culminating in bonfires of their contents also continued for several days.[2] There can be little doubt that the disorder in London helped to persuade many that there was no alternative but to hasten the coming of the prince of Orange and the renewal of effective government. 'All the Lords and city', wrote a correspondent of Abigail Harley's on 13 December, 'have invited the Prince of Orange which we all pray may come quickly that a stop may be put to the fury of the rabble who have done great mischief.'[3] Other private correspondence of the times shows similar fears of the mob—fears which were heightened by rumours of depredations by the disbanded Irish troops.[4] A clash between the latter and the townsmen of Reading gave some verisimilitude to these fears.[5]

These rumours were not confined to London. At Oxford, where an anti-papist riot had already taken place on 4 December, it was rumoured two days later that the king's dragoons were coming to plunder the city and university, and Magdalen bridge was pulled down as a defensive measure.[6] Even in Lancashire and Cheshire it was believed that Irish troops were marching north plundering and burning en route.[7] The mob gave free vent to their hatred for the catholics. The rioting in Cambridge, already referred to, continued until nearly the end of the month.[8] In various parts of the country attacks were made on the houses of noblemen and others prominent on the catholic side, under the pretext of searching for 'priests, arms, and horses'.[9] The fittings of private chapels and household furniture were

---

[1] H.M.C. le Fleming, p. 226; Reresby Memoirs, pp. 537–8; Autobiography of Sir John Bramston, pp. 339–40; An Account of the Manner of taking the Lord Chancellor Jeffreys, Bodley, fol. θ, 590 (44).

[2] Portledge Papers, p. 52.   [3] H.M.C. Portland, iii. 420.

[4] Latimer, p. 488.   [5] Hatton Correspondence, ii. 121–7.

[6] Wood, Life and Times, iii. 286–7.   [7] H.M.C. le Fleming, p. 229.

[8] Ibid., p. 226. See also Alderman Samuel Newton's diary, ed. Foster 1890, pp. 96–7, where there is a vivid description of the panic in Cambridge caused by the rumoured approach of the Irish troops.

[9] e.g. at York. Reresby Memoirs, p. 531.

destroyed, at least one catholic's house burned, and in places park-pales torn down and the deer seized. Northampton-shire, Cambridgeshire, Norfolk, and Suffolk appear to have been the chief centres of rioting, but similar incidents were also reported from counties as far apart as Kent and West-morland.[1] In the midlands such was the disorder that soldiers were detailed in Leicestershire to assist the collectors of excise and chimney money, but by 19 December things had become quiet enough for it to be seen that they would not after all be needed, and for the county's militia to be dismissed.[2]

Even the assumption of authority by the new sovereigns could not at once put an end to the prevailing disorders. And such incidents as the mutiny at Ipswich in April 1689 must be viewed against the background of a country which had as yet by no means achieved internal peace.[3] Shropshire, for instance, appears to have been particularly disturbed, and in February and May there were petitions to the secretary of state, for protection against riotous mobs.[4] Similar petitions came in April from the earl of Cardigan from Northamptonshire, and from Worcestershire in May and June.[5]

In Newcastle in May, a riot, apparently incited by the military, had as its object the destruction of the statue of James II, on the plea that 'our laws, liberties, and properties were taken away and all by that statue'.[6]

The confiscation of weapons held by supposed adherents

---

[1] Luttrell, i. 490; *H.M.C. le Fleming*, pp. 228–31; *Portledge Papers*, p. 56.

[2] *H.M.C. Cowper*, ii. 345. Leicestershire appears to have been one of the few counties where the militia was called out during the Revolution—but the 'un-official' calling to the prince's standard would account for the activities of much the same class. The W. Riding Militia which had been called out in the middle of November went over to Danby on the 22nd. *Reresby Memoirs*, pp. 523–31. The Riding remained remarkably quiet, in spite of the absence of legal authority, and comparatively free from crime. Ibid., pp. 542–3.

[3] *C.S.P. Dom., 1689–90*, pp. 57–8; A. Grey, *Debates of the House of Commons*, ix. 164–9.

[4] *H.M.C. Portland*, iii. 426; *C.S.P. Dom., 1689–90*, pp. 4 and 110. The trouble in Shropshire started in January, when it was rumoured that the Convention was going to recall James. This was said to have the effect of damping the market. *H.M.C. Portland*, iii. 421 and 432. See also *infra*, p. 58.

[5] *C.S.P. Dom., 1689–90*, pp. 54, 95, and 167.

[6] Ibid., pp. 111 and 115; *H.M.C. Cowper*, ii. 355–6.

of the catholic religion or the legitimist cause, which was soon, as we shall see, to become a regular part of the machinery of order, was now carried on locally by adherents of the new régime, and in some places occasioned further disorder.

Lord Delamere once more was particularly active in Cheshire, and once more his activity appears not to have been wholly uninfluenced by such personal matters as the non-fulfilment of his wishes in parliamentary elections. The drilling of the militia was made the excuse for tumultuous assemblies in Cheshire and Lancashire whose watchword was 'for the King and Lord Delamere', and it was noted with apprehension that among those summoning the people of Manchester to appear was the son of one of Oliver Cromwell's marshals. There appears to be no record of any actual disorder committed by these gatherings, but so universal was the apprehension caused by them that it was said that even the approach of William's fleet, in the previous November, had not made a 'greater buzz' in those parts.[1]

After the Boyne and La Hogue, the new régime appeared to have reached at least temporary stability. But the fear of Jacobite plotting remained fixed in the minds of the statesmen of William's reign. To successive secretaries of state, the fact that, over large areas, sections of the population were in a state bordering on destitution, was as nothing compared with the news that some informer, as generous with irrelevant detail as he was almost always untrustworthy, had observed in some tavern in the purlieus of Drury Lane the gathering of three or four dismissed officers of James's army or had overheard in Hyde Park the conversation of a masked lady and a gentleman with a Scottish accent.[2]

This aspect of the reign is continuous and scarcely varies with the changes in the political situation. An interesting account might be given, too, of the police activities of this régime, which plays so prominent a part in the history of

[1] *H.M.C. Finch*, ii. 210–11. Who the 'marshal's son' was is not stated. It might apply to the son of any Cromwellian officer.

[2] The richest source for the accounts of informers about the various plots against William III is the correspondence of the secretary of state, Sir William Trumbull, calendared in *H.M.C. Downshire*, i.

British liberties. Much governmental energy was spent in searching for and arresting suspects and in controlling the expression of opinion in writing or by word of mouth. But it would be found that on the whole respect for the forms of law was carefully maintained, and that the conduct of ministers compares not unfavourably with that of other governments at other times, whose security has been menaced by secret plotting, with assassination not excluded from among its weapons.

A list of those indicted for seditious words and of the remarks which caused their arrest would not be without its humorous side.[1] But these activities, important enough in themselves and in their effect on the public mind, are outside our main field because this subversive activity singularly failed to find an outlet in popular disorder. The conspiracy in Lancashire and Cheshire, which was the great political feature of 1694, produced nothing of this kind except for a certain display of popular feeling when the trials of the alleged conspirators took place.[2] The Jacobites failed to make political capital out of the very severe economic distress of the middle years of the reign. Even in its beginnings, Jacobitism was not a popular movement.

We shall have to deal here, then, only with the very few occasions when the valour of the Jacobites got the better of their discretion.

The frequent rescue of prisoners has already been referred to as proof of the weaknesses of the administration. In July 1690 the news that the French had landed in the west caused the disaffected element at Morpeth to break open the jail and release certain imprisoned suspects.[3] An attack on the Savoy prison in London in April 1695 enabled some prisoners in custody for high treason to escape.[4] The most notorious of attempts of that kind was, however, the one made in May of the same year, when, on the 27th, an endeavour was made to rescue some prisoners from a messenger's house there. A further riot by 'some drunken gentlemen' the next

---

[1] The Hertford Gaol Calendar for 1697 contains the entry: 'Wm. Armstronge, charged with having a counterfeit pass and a paper of Jacobite verses, reflecting on the present government and also suspected of having stolen a watch.' *Hertford County Records*, i. 430. [2] Luttrell, iii. 393; Macaulay, v. 550–1.
[3] Luttrell, ii. 86. [4] *C.S.P. Dom., 1694–5*, p. 435.

day was believed to have the same end in view. The government was seriously worried by this, as the civil authorities had been unaccountably slack, and as the officer who commanded the guard had allowed five of the rioters to depart on parole.[1]

Rejoicings at public events also provided a recognized opportunity for disorders. The people of Stamford celebrated the coronation of William and Mary by feasting out of doors. The mayor and other disaffected persons retaliated by sending for the fire-engine and the militia. The soldiers threatened to shoot 'the presbyterian rogues' and played the engine on to the crowd. And, instead of honouring the loyal toast, the mayor and the parson drank to the 'old gentleman'. The mayor and his brothers were subsequently arrested.[2] Resentment was shown, too, at Carlisle in November 1697 against the rejoicings at the peace, when the mob threatened to break windows which had been illuminated. These feelings can scarcely be described, however, as spontaneous, as money had previously been offered with the aid of which King James's health might be drunk.[3] No doubt similar incidents of a riotous nature accompanied other public expressions of joy or grief—incidents whose only record is an indictment for seditious words.

Occasionally the Jacobites would rejoice openly at events which they considered propitious for their cause—at Bath in July 1693, at the news of a defeat of William in Flanders,[4] and in Bristol at the news of Queen Mary's death.[5]

The most notable riot, however, was the one occasioned by the rejoicings of the Jacobites on the anniversary of the prince of Wales's birth on 10 June 1695. The prince's health was openly drunk with musical accompaniments in

[1] *C.S.P. Dom.*, *1694–5*, pp. 479 and 483; *1695*, p. 341; Luttrell, iii. 494–5; *H.M.C. Downshire*, i. 472. It was not only the Jacobites who were believed capable of rescuing prisoners. In May 1701 it was believed that an attempt would be made to rescue those committed to the Gatehouse prison for presenting the Kentish petition, and precautions were duly taken. *Parliamentary History*, v. 1251–7.

[2] *C.S.P. Dom.*, *1689–90*, pp. 61, 68, 123.

[3] P.C. 2. 77, pp. 117 and 123.

[4] *C.S.P. Dom.*, *1693*, pp. 251 and 272.

[5] *Portledge Papers*, p. 192.

several places in London. The Jacobites gathered at the Dog Tavern in Drury Lane went further and attempted to make passers-by join in their celebrations. This caused a riot in which the loyal mob eventually put to flight the Jacobites. Some of the latter were arrested.[1] A few days later the lord mayor and aldermen of the city, as well as the Middlesex justices, were sent for to Whitehall and told to take care for the future to prevent such riotous meetings.[2]

The year 1696, filled though it was with rumours of plots against the government and the king, and with trials for treason, seems, possibly because of the alertness of the administration, to have been singularly free from disorder in the capital, apart from tumults caused by the scarcity of coin. On 6 June Lapthorne wrote: 'Affairs are quiet, here, thanks be to God but we had more than ordinary guards out these Holidays, fearing lest the mob might have been mutinous.'[3] The perpetual revelation of new plots, the measures of the government to control the movements of the disaffected, the searches for suspects and for weapons, all, however, assisted to maintain the fear of an outbreak. On 16 November Alice Coke wrote from Parsloe in Essex to Thomas Coke at Melbourne in Derbyshire:

'Dear Brother, You are happy that you are quietly taking your recreation in the country and only hear at a distance of tumults and bustles that are every minute in the town. Sometimes there's a report sent abroad that a hundred and twenty blunderbusses are ready charged to kill his Majesty. Immediately upon this all the gates of the city are shut and all that can't give an account of themselves are clapped up till they can and then set at liberty again . . . I was at London yesterday and am so tired of hearing of nothing but disorder and tumults and hurrying into prison and letting out again that I almost made a resolution to go no more this winter.'[4]

Of other open Jacobite rioting the period seems to have been free. From the accession of Anne onwards, the attention

---

[1] *C.S.P. Dom., 1694–5*, pp. 493–4, and *1697*, p. 192; Luttrell, iii. 483–93; *Portledge Papers*, p. 205. For the efforts of the Jacobites to save these rioters, and those concerned in the Haymarket riot of the previous month, by postponing the trial and removing or bribing witnesses, see *H.M.C. Downshire*, i. 472–94 and 540.

[2] Luttrell, iii. 495.

[3] *Portledge Papers*, p. 232.   [4] *H.M.C. Cowper*, ii. 366–7.

of the malcontents was directed rather to preparing the way for her brother peacefully to succeed her.[1]

Occasionally, isolated incidents throw light on this underground activity, which was not confined by any means to those leading statesmen whose clandestine correspondence with the exiled king has afforded so many themes for history and fiction. In the years 1706–8 a certain amount of publicity was achieved by a sect of foreigners calling themselves the French prophets, whose open-air devotions caused riotous mobs to assemble in the capital upon several occasions, notably on 1 May 1707, when they attempted to restore a dead body to life in St. Paul's churchyard.[2] There appears to have been a more dangerous side to their activities, for a report of October 1708 suggests that they were engaged in disseminating Jacobite propaganda.[3]

The hospitality of the government to religious refugees from abroad caused trouble on more than one occasion. In September 1683 there was a riot directed against the French protestant colony at Norwich under the impression that it was in fact one of catholics.[4] The arrival in 1708–9 of thousands of the fleeing subjects of the Elector Palatine put too much strain on the national goodwill, especially since it appeared that the genuineness of the destitution and of the protestantism of some of their number was more than suspect.[5] Not only were they accused, as was natural, of destroying the livelihood of native workers, but they were also suspected of having brought in the small-pox.[6] An attempt to settle some of them at Sundridge in Kent, in October 1709, caused some disorder, and the popular hatred of them provided a theme for the Sacheverell rioters.[7]

Meanwhile the mob was still being made use of in the strife of parties. In February 1689 an attempt was made to force the Convention to offer William the crown by the staging of a popular petition, the party desiring this having

[1] The Jacobites were not even credited, except by the more obscure pamphleteers, with any share in promoting the Sacheverell riots. J. H. Burton, *A History of the Reign of Queen Anne*, ii. 285.   [2] Ibid., pp. 341–5.
[3] *H.M.C. Marlborough*, p. 46.   [4] *C.S.P. Dom.*, *1683* (2), p. 363.
[5] G. M. Trevelyan, *England under Queen Anne*, iii, 1934, pp. 35–9.
[6] *H.M.C. Portland*, iv. 549.
[7] C.S.P. Dom., Anne, MS. p. 534; Trevelyan, iii. 38.

'sent some instruments to stir up the mobile'.[1] Thereafter, though occasional attempts were made at the tumultuous petitioning of parliament, it was chiefly in elections that the mob intervened. Successive election campaigns took on a character more and more violent, though in the absence of any social or economic issues the rioters' own interests were scarcely involved in the outcome.[2]

Rioting was rendered easier by the practice of removing troops from towns where they were quartered for the duration of the elections.[3] The violent intimidation of the electorate with the aid of hired mobs was recognized by both parties as a means of gaining votes. The whig paper *The Flying Post* drew up after the election of 1710 a mock bill of the costs of a 'late Tory election in the West'. This included items such as 'for bespeaking and collecting a mob £20; for Roarers of the word Church £40, for a set of No-Roundhead Roarers £40', and further sums for 'demolishing two houses' and 'committing two riots'.[4]

The first notable election riots occurred in 1695 at Westminster and Exeter, among other places.[5] Wood records an election riot at Oxford on 23 September, 'mostly provoked by the town-clerk, Slatford'.[6] The conditions making for disorder can clearly be seen when we read of the election of 1698, at Westminster, that two of the candidates appeared in Tuthill Fields on polling-day with about 2,000 mounted followers. Their sole opponent could only muster 200 horsemen, but they were followed by 'a great number of the rabble on foot'.[7]

The election of 1705 was notorious for the amount of disorder to which it gave rise. The scene of the worst rioting was Coventry. There the mayor and aldermen, on receipt of a letter from Harley, then secretary of state, drew up an order that no strangers should meddle in the election and forbidding voters to carry clubs, sticks, and weapons. Some of the aldermen refused to join in these measures, and the

---

[1] *Reresby Memoirs*, pp. 548–9.
[2] Trevelyan, *England under the Stuarts*, ed. of 1930, p. 472.
[3] *Infra*, Chap. VII. E. Handasyde mentions in her *Granville the Polite*, p. 130, the billeting of troops upon electors as a means of influencing recalcitrant votes.
[4] Quoted C. M. Clode, *The Military Forces of the Crown*, 1889, i. 121.
[5] Macaulay, vi. 82.   [6] Anthony Wood, *Life and Times*, ed. A. Clark, 1891, iii. 489.   [7] *C.S.P. Dom., 1698*, p. 365.

two sheriffs, as well as some of the constables, were backward in performing their respective duties. Appeals to the candidates to preserve the peace were unsuccessful as far as one party was concerned.

On the night when trouble was anticipated the mayor and some of the aldermen sat up all night with the constables and watch, who were ordered not to use their staves and halberds but to apprehend breakers of the peace. Awareness of this latter order appears to have emboldened the rioters, who appeared at about 3 a.m. under the leadership of one of the candidates and attacked the forces of the law by hurling stones and brickbats.

The ensuing riot lasted for several hours and resulted in the triumph of the rioters, who at 9 a.m. possessed themselves of the town hall with six or seven hundred men, and retained it for the three days of the election. This enabled them to deal as they pleased with the voters, many of whom were severely assaulted.[1]

Robert Price, a baron of the exchequer who held the assizes there in August 1706, had no easy task, since he had to deal with nearly 150 persons who had been indicted for rioting at the election. Nor was his work rendered easier by the appearance, on the occasion of the trial, of the rival candidates and their supporting mobs. He was eventually able to report to Harley, however, that some measure of conciliation had been achieved.[2] The election was not unnaturally declared void.[3]

Coventry, although interesting in view of the survival of so detailed an account of the riots, was not the only place so favoured. At Chester the whigs broke the windows of the cathedral and of another church.[4] Defoe reported to Harley the 'strange insults' received by the dukes of Bolton and Somerset at the hands of the Salisbury mob, and described the election at Honiton as 'an abridgement of Coventry'.[5]

Meanwhile hatred of the government and of the dis-

[1] H.M.C. Portland, iv. 187–8; C.J. xv. 276–8.
[2] H.M.C. Portland, iv. 320. Why so long should have elapsed before the trials is difficult to understand, but it shows the long survival of the party feud.
[3] Luttrell, vi. 135.
[4] H.M.C. Portland, iv. 189.   [5] Ibid., pp. 213 and 270.

senters who were among the government's chief supporters was growing. Earlier incidents had shown how the popular animosity against the catholics could, in this period when they were far from prominent, be transferred to the more numerous and affluent body. The news of Anne's accession had led, at Newcastle under Lyme, to the destruction of meeting-houses.[1] These scenes were now, under the impetus given by the Sacheverell prosecution, to be transferred on a greater scale to the metropolis.

The attacks on the dissenters' meeting-houses and the other manifestations of the tory sympathies of the populace have been fully treated by all historians of Anne's reign, and there is little to add.[2]

The problem as to how far they were spontaneous and how far deliberately stirred up is still unsolved. The whig pamphleteers asserted that the mobs were hired.[3] Tories replied that, on the contrary, the whigs rather than themselves were responsible, since mob violence was the natural expression of whig principles. A people who were told that there was a right of resistance, that 'they were the original of government', would naturally act accordingly. True tories abhorred all tumults, even those favouring their own side.[4]

The really violent whigs seemed to admit the indictment and only regret that the mob had on this occasion been led astray, it was not quite clear by whom.

'Is this a cause for freeborn Subjects to engage in?' wrote one of them. 'I am asham'd and griev'd that such slavish Souls should dishonour the name and title of Mobb. But you are the first and I hope will be the last Mobb, that ever stood up against Liberty and Property [sic], and the freedom of the subject. You a Mobb! You are the Scum and Dregs, the Tools and Vassals of the Romish Breed and sent from their dark Hellish Cabals once more if you could to blow up Queen and Parliament.'[5]

On the other side recrimination went as far as the sugges-

[1] F. W. Wyon, History of the Reign of Queen Anne, 1876, i. 73.
[2] The fullest treatment is in J. H. Burton's History of the Reign of Queen Anne, 1880. A contemporary account is A. Boyer's in Annals of the Reign of Queen Anne, Eighth Year, pp. 264–71.
[3] W. Bisset, The Modern Fanatick, preface (Bodley Pamph. 285. 52).
[4] A Vindication of Dr. Sacheverell, p. 9 (Bodley Pamph. 285. 53).
[5] Letter from Captain Tom to the Mobb now Rais'd for Dr. Sacheverell (Bodley Pamph. 285. 30).

tion that the whigs had promoted the disturbances in order to benefit from the expected reaction in their favour. 'I'll tell you just the same that they proposed from Daniel Defoe's Shortest Way with Dissenters.'[1]

Whether or not there was any truth in this, Burnet also suspected 'secret management in the matter', because no attempt was made to prosecute any papists or non-jurors who were mentioned in the proclamation of 2 March as the chief promoters of the riots, beyond the order, usual at moments of political excitement, for the departure of all papists from the capital.[2] Interesting, too, is the suspicion, voiced by Abigail Harley on 7 March, when the mob had been dispersed, that they might have been at first 'had the government so desired it'. This was not the only time in the course of several letters when she voiced this suspicion. Indeed, she wrote further that she believed that it was only the fact that some ministers had been personally insulted and that they felt themselves in danger that induced them to act at all: 'somebody talking to Lord Wharton about the dissenters, he said he did not care if they were all damned'.[3] Yet it is difficult to see what the government could hope to gain out of the riots, unless they hoped that the concentration of interest upon the dissenters would remove it from themselves.

Whatever accusations of negligence can be made against the ministers, it is clear at least, in spite of the pamphleteers, that neither they nor any other set of people deliberately organized the riots.

'Anyone', writes Burton, 'who with some practical acquaintance with criminal inquiries reads the abundant documents making up the trials for high treason on this occasion, sees at once that the failure to reach the leaders was not caused by the deep policy of this organization, but by the absence of all organization, and the ephemeral wayward nature of the motions of an unorganized mob.'[4]

---

[1] A Vindication of Dr. Sacheverell, p. 11.

[2] Burnet, iv. 283–4. Cf. Burton, ii. 250. For the proclamation see Crawford, p. 531; P.C. 2. 82, pp. 544–6. A motion to insert 'Republicans' as well as papists and non-jurors in the address of the commons to the queen requesting the issue of the proclamation, was defeated by 114 votes to 79. Luttrell, vi. 552; Boyer, p. 269.

[3] H.M.C. Portland, iv. 533–44.

[4] Burton, ii. 254. Boyer mentions the suspicion that the riots were deliberately contrived, but says 'of this no legal proof having been made, History cannot record it for truth'. Op. cit., p. 267.

If, indeed, we read the trials of Dammaree, the waterman, of Willis and Purchase, remembering the strength of political and religious passion prevailing at the time, the years of poverty caused by the slack trade of the war period, the animosity towards the 'Palatines' and to those who had allowed them to come, and, most important of all, the readiness of the London mob to resort to violence especially when under the influence of drink, we need look no farther for the causes of the disturbances.[1]

The effort of the attorney-general to prove the design to have been a deep-laid one for the destruction of all meeting-houses, and hence treasonable, depended upon making out a riotous assembly in the Temple, in which no doubt the popular catchwords were shouted, to have been a meeting of conspirators for the formulation of plans.[2]

The continuance of the disturbances after the date of the attack on the meeting-houses suggests, too, that the disorders were the spontaneous outcome of discontent. On 17 March, more than two weeks after the original riot, a further proclamation called attention to the persistence of disorder and ordered sufficient watch and ward to be kept in London.[3] On 28 March Luttrell records that a letter has been sent by the queen to the lord mayor ordering him to take measures for the preservation of the peace, and if necessary to call the military to his assistance for this purpose. A court of lieutenancy therefore ordered four companies of the train-bands to keep guard every night.[4] In the middle of the next month the justices of Middlesex were ordered by Sunderland, the secretary of state, to prevent 'seditious libels', which stirred up the mob, from being cried about the streets.'[5]

The rioting in the provinces which followed the promulgation of the sentence can scarcely be termed organized.

---

[1] *State Trials*, viii. 219–67, and ibid., App., pp. 552–7. An anticipated attack on the bank did not materialize, possibly because it was known that regular troops had been sent. Ibid., p. 224; Burton, p. 253; Luttrell, vi. 551–4; Rapin and Tindal, *History of England*, ed. of 1743–5, IV. i. 155.　　　[2] *State Trials*, viii. 222.

[3] P.C. 2. 83, p. 398. Ten days later the court of aldermen appointed a committee to investigate the riots. Offenders were bound over to the sessions. Sharpe, *London and the Kingdom*, 1894–5, ii. 635.

[4] Luttrell, vi. 262; Rapin and Tindal, IV. i. 156.　　　[5] Ibid., p. 572.

That at Oxford is sufficiently explained by the notorious high-tory inclinations of the university.[1] Elsewhere the clergy of Sacheverell's way of thought helped to rouse the mob by violent sermons.[2]

On the administrative side, the Sacheverell riots serve once more to show the inadequacy of the ordinary civilian machinery for the preservation of order, which was recognized in the proclamation of 17 March to which we have referred. One of the military witnesses at Dammaree's trial gave an explicit account of the helplessness of a constable and of some of the watch whom he met, who dared not do anything, being in fear of their lives.[3]

The riots on 1 March were suppressed by the use of the regular troops, the horse and foot guards sent by the queen in spite of more timid advice from those who feared for the safety of the palace. The part played by the train-bands is more doubtful. Boyer writes that on 2 March the train-bands of London and Westminster were called to arms 'and placed in divers Posts, where they continued as long as Dr. Sacheverell's trial was depending: which both lessen'd the number of mutineers (many of the said train'd bands being men of low degree hired by substantial housekeepers) and kept the rest in Awe'.[4] Burton emphatically describes them as useless. This seems to be an exaggeratedly pessimistic view. Once the riot had been quelled, it was to them that the preservation of order was entrusted, and, as we have seen, their services were requisitioned again later in the month.[5] Their chief defect seems to have been a slow rate of mobilization. Abigail Harley remarks that when the mob tried to proceed to the city from Drury Lane 'the weavers rose and then the train-bands, and so frustrated their design'.[6]

By the time of the election of 1710, enthusiasm in the

---

[1] *H.M.C. Portland*, iv. 532 and 539.

[2] There is a letter from Wrexham of 4 April regretting that the fomenting of the outrages of those parts must be attributed to some of the clergy. C.S.P. Dom., Anne, MS. p. 565. At Ely there was an anti-Sacheverell riot. The rioters' slogan was 'noe Church, noe oaths, no Prince of Wales'. State Papers, Anne, 37 (nos. 157, 161 (?)).

[3] *State Trials*, viii. 223.   [4] Boyer, pp. 266–7.

[5] Luttrell, vi. 551; Burton, ii. 252–3.   [6] *H.M.C. Portland*, iv. 532.

country on either side had reached its height. The flood
of pamphlet literature continued unabated. The result was
the most riotous election campaign of the period. If we
may trust a partisan, the roads had been rendered unsafe,
'especially since matters were ripening for the election by
drunken Zealots crying High Church, High Church'.[1] The
election itself was marked by riots at London, Westminster,
Southwark, Liverpool, Chester, Northwich, Marlow, Whit-
church, Coventry, Chippenham, and Newark.[2] Finally, the
London mob, rejoicing at the tory victory, broke all unillumi-
nated windows, including those of the successful candidate.[3]

In order to bring the narrative of political disorder down
to the passing of the Riot Act, it is necessary to mention
the extensive rioting which occurred on the occasion of
George I's coronation, and during the ensuing election.[4] It
was thus political rioting, not popular tumults due to economic causes, which finally brought about a strengthening
of the law. Nevertheless, the two were still inseparable. For
instance, in the summer of 1715 the efforts of the Jacobites
to create disturbance were aided by the fact that discontent
had been created by the government's refusal to continue
a subsidy to farmers who had sustained losses through a
cattle plague.[5]

[1] Bisset, *The Modern Fanatick*, pp. 7–9.
[2] W. T. Morgan, 'An Eighteenth Century Election in England', *The Political
Science Quarterly*, vol. 37, especially pp. 593–5; Rapin and Tindal, IV. i. 193;
Picton, ii. 4.
[3] *Parliamentary History*, vi. 917.
[4] 1 Geo. I, Sess. 2, cap. 5; Lecky, i. 261–2.
[5] W. Michael, *The Beginnings of the Hanoverian Dynasty*, 1936, p. 132.

III

THE FOOD SUPPLY

THE examination of the laws relating to the import and export of corn in the period between 1555 and 1663 leads our most recent authority to the conclusion that 'the policy of protecting the producer masked a consistent determination to safeguard the consumer'; and, although the restrictions on export might be avoided by the manipulation of the market, the attempts made by the government to enforce them were both determined and in part successful.[1] The medieval restrictions upon the internal trade in foodstuffs were also continued into this period, and in times of great scarcity special measures to ensure the corn supply of the poorer elements in the population were taken by municipal authorities and county justices, acting often on the express instructions of the central government. These measures varied from the imposing of restrictions on the use of grain for brewing to the purchase by local authorities of stocks of corn to be either sold at special prices to the poor or else thrown on to the market in times of scarcity in order to depress general prices. These measures were no doubt largely dictated by the fear of popular disorder, for a population so dependent on home-grown corn was liable to take violent action when prices rose. Such years as 1527, 1551, 1587, 1596, 1622–3, and 1630 saw widespread disorder and attacks on dealers and others suspected of hoarding corn.[2]

Of such disturbances the later Stuart period provides many instances. It is true that the corn-riots of this period never assumed severe enough proportions seriously to alarm the government. Nor were they even responsible for a flow of pamphlet literature on the subject of the corn laws such as followed upon the severe rioting of 1756.[3] It is, indeed, very

---

[1] Lipson, ii. 448–553.

[2] Leonard, especially chaps. viii–x.

[3] D. G. Barnes, *A History of the English Corn Laws*, 1930, pp. 31–2. The author remarks that he has found no pamphlet published between 1660 and 1750 dealing exclusively with the corn laws; a remarkable fact in an age exceptionally prolific in economic pamphleteers. Op. cit., p. 16.

often difficult to connect directly the ameliorative efforts of the slow-moving administration with the violent manifestations of popular discontent of which we have record. Indeed, the chief interest of these disturbances lies rather in the illustration they provide of the popular attitude to what a recent historian has rightly called 'a little-known revolution in our fiscal policy'—a revolution which resulted in the overthrow in England first among all the important European states of the medieval policy of 'provision' in favour of the free or even bounty-encouraged export of food-stuffs and raw material.[1]

The responsibility for the new policy must be sought in that alliance between the landowning and mercantile classes which has been noted as the outstanding fact of the social structure of mercantilist England. It is not hard to see who were the immediate benefactors of the new policy. 'I hope', wrote one country gentleman, in September 1708, 'the dearth of corn which is likely to continue for several years to come will make husbandry very profitable to us, in breaking up and improving all our new land, which is now overrun with bushes or at least it will bring us good tenants to take leases and give good rates for our farms.'[2]

By the side of these improving landlords we must place the merchants and shipowners who benefited from the export trade in corn. Indeed, the clause making the bounty only payable when the corn was exported in British ships meant, as Andrew Marvell wrote, 'the incouragement of our own navigation having prevailed against that of the landowners after several long debates'.[3] Since these classes were those politically dominant, it is not surprising that the government of Charles II should have been willing to experiment with the bounty, and that the Revolution government

[1] Edward Hughes, *E.H.R.* li, 1936, p. 339.
[2] Robert Molesworth of Edlington, Yorkshire. *H.M.C. Var. Coll.* viii. 239. In 1710 he recorded with satisfaction that prices were likely to rise, since the reported plague in the Baltic would send the Dutch to England for their supplies. Ibid., p. 249.
[3] *Letters of A. Marvell*, pp. 132–3, referring to a bounty bill which apparently passed the Commons in 1671 without reaching the statute book. The speculative transactions made possible by the bounty had an unfavourable effect on the home supply. R. B. Westerfield, *Middlemen in English Business, 1660–1760*, 1915, pp. 161–9.

should have aimed in the act of 1689 at conciliating them by putting on a more permanent footing the system of export bounties.[1] Indeed, the statesmen of this period were more alarmed than ever they were by food-riots, by the thought of the possible political consequences of years of low corn prices when, as in Shropshire in 1690, 'the noise of taxes and the deadness of markets filled the country with complaints'.[2]

Before concluding that the new corn laws did indeed bear that major share of responsibility for the recurrent periods of scarcity which they were assigned in the popular mind, a more detailed examination of the period is called for. We must endeavour to place in their correct context such disturbances as did clearly arise out of the deficiencies in the food supply.[3]

The early years of the Restoration were years of fairly high prices. There is little evidence of any large-scale export of corn, though some export licences were issued.[4] Even a small amount was sufficient, however, to arouse local discontent. In December 1662 there was a riot at Sherborne; in February 1663 there was rioting in Southampton, in the next month at Wareham in Dorset, and in May at Christchurch in Hampshire.[5]

The act of 1663 altered the scale of prices which controlled exports and the import duties, since it had been rendered out of date by the rise in prices.[6] This made no immediate difference to the situation. Some corn was still exported under licence, and in May 1666 and September 1667 there were proclamations completely freeing the export of food-stuffs in view of the prevalent low prices.[7] The period of low prices continued, and there was during these

---

[1] Stats. of Realm, 25 Car. II, cap. 1, cl. 31; Stats. of Realm, 1 Will. & Mar. cap. 12. Cf. N. S. B. Gras, *The Evolution of the English Corn Market*, 1915, pp. 144–6 and 253–4.　　　　　　　　　　[2] *H.M.C. Portland*, liii. 442.

[3] For a table of corn prices in these years, see the figures taken from Lord Ernle's book in the Appendix. But it must be remembered that an annual average market price calculated from the figures of two market days tends to conceal the violence of the fluctuations in price which were so important to the poorer classes.

[4] Gras, p. 113; *C.S.P. Dom.*, *1660–1*, p. 383; *1661–2*, p. 621.

[5] Ibid., p. 602; *1663–4*, p. 130; P.C. 2. 56, pp. 317 and 344.

[6] Stats. of Realm, 15 Car. II, cap. 7; Barnes, p. 9.

[7] Stats. of Realm, 15 Car. II, cap. 7; *C.S.P. Dom.*, *1664–5*, pp. 198 and 207; *1665–6*, p. 391; *1666–7*, pp. 261 and 362; *1667–8*, p. 456.

years little evidence of scarcity at home in spite of the damage done to coastwise shipping by Dutch privateers during the war. This was severe enough to necessitate a convoy system, and in 1667 the depredations of the French caused actual scarcity in the Channel islands.[1] Meanwhile the efforts to control the internal corn trade in the interests of the consumer had not wholly ceased. After some negotiation a group headed by Sir Richard Mauleverer obtained in 1663 a warrant for putting into force the laws against forestallers and engrossers. They were apparently to act as informers (without restraining others from doing likewise) and were to be recompensed by the grant of half the fines exacted from the law-breakers they discovered. This peculiar arrangement was continued for a further five years by a warrant of July 1664.[2]

It was, however, the lowness of prices, not their excessive height, which troubled the administration, and there was considerable anxiety shown about the methods to be adopted to prevent importation of corn. This was totally prohibited by a proclamation of March 1669.[3] Administrative measures alone proved insufficient and the result was the legislation of 1670 and 1673.[4] The first of these enactments permitted exportation at all times on the payment of duty and introduced a sliding scale for imports, and the second introduced for the first time the principle of the bounty. According to Gras the bounty payable under the act was in fact only paid during two one-year periods, from Michaelmas 1674 to Michaelmas 1675, and again from Michaelmas 1680 to Michaelmas 1681. Its total effect cannot accurately be measured, but there was certainly a marked expansion of exports in the period 1675–7, which seems only partly due to the demand created by the war in Holland.[5] In 1674, a year of high prices, there had been a corn-riot at Stratford on Avon and sluices on the river were broken to prevent the

[1] Ibid., 1666–7, pp. 434, 571, 580, 596.
[2] Ibid., 1663–4, pp. 253, 329, 336, 372, 642. A few years later Sir Richard is found at the head of a group made commissioners for licensing and regulating hackney coaches. Ibid., 1667–8, p. 358.
[3] Ibid., 1668, pp. 450, 462, 516, 522; 1669, pp. 233, 252.
[4] Stats. of Realm, 22 Car. II, cap. 13, and 25 Car. II, cap. I, cl. 31.
[5] Gras, pp. 113–14; Lipson, ii. 453.

corn-laden barges from moving.[1] In the autumn of 1675
the correspondence of Williamson, the secretary of state,
contained accounts of the shipping of a large amount of
corn from Falmouth, Truro, and Bridlington. This was
ascribed to the Bounty Act by Williamson's informants,
who warned him that people were beginning to murmur at
the rising prices. In the winter of 1676–7 corn continued
to be exported from Bridlington, and large sums to be paid
out in bounties.[2] In June 1681 there was again a corn-riot,
this time at Reading, and it was aggravated by the refusal of
the mayor to assist the dealer who was being attacked.[3]

The act of 1689 was, as we have seen, a natural outcome
of the new government's desire to conciliate the landowning
class, which had been hit by the low prices of the years
immediately preceding and following the Revolution. It
was not until 1692 that the first bad harvest of the reign
occurred. In November the arrival of some Dutch factors
to buy up corn at Colchester caused some disturbance.[4] In
the following February Luttrell recorded further trouble at
several unspecified places.[5] Colchester itself was apparently
troublesome again in the spring, when it was one of the
places whose authorities received special instructions to
suppress the riots.[6]

The instructions referred to were in the form of letters
from the council to the mayors of Colchester, Worcester,
and Shrewsbury, accompanied by instructions to the lord-
lieutenants of the respective counties to render assistance.
'Whereas', ran the council's letter of 4 May 1693, it had
'received information that severall Persons' had 'lately
assembled themselves in a riotous and tumultuous manner
in that city under a false and scandalous pretence that Corn
is bought up to be sent or exported into France', they required
the mayor to suppress the riots according to the statutes
usually cited and to punish those found guilty of them.[7]

---

[1] P.C. 2. 64, pp. 224 and 280.
[2] *C.S.P. Dom.*, *1675–6*, pp. 377–8, 403, 433; *1676–7*, pp. 414 and 498.
[3] P.C. 2. 69, p. 312.   [4] Luttrell, ii. 629.
[5] Luttrell, ii. 20 and 32.   [6] P.C. 2. 75, pp. 146–7.
[7] The statutes referred to were those of 15 Ric. II and 13 Henry IV. P.C. 2,
loc. cit. J. Noake, in *Worcestershire in Olden Times*, 1849, refers to the riot as
taking place in about 1691.

Whether or not the pretence that corn was destined for France was 'false and scandalous', it seems clear that the immediate cause of the first riot in Worcester (on 30 April) was the arrival of some factors 'to buy up corne, bacon and cheese to export them'. The factors and their barges were attacked. The mayor succeeded at first in dispersing the rioters and in arresting the ringleaders. But on the following day the mob, to the number, it was asserted, of 200, broke open the jail, assaulted the constables, and proceeded out of the city to plunder a granary some four miles away. Their absence gave the mayor an opportunity, of which he made use, to summon the militia. Ten days later, however, the mob broke out again and plundered another granary.[1]

For the root of the trouble here, we must look not merely to the prevailing high prices, but to a particular local grievance, the depressed state of the cloth industry.[2] The grievance was set forth in a document which appears quoted in a presentment for seditious libel made to the commission which tried the rioters. The document is imperfect, but the gist can be clearly followed. The writer complains that distress has been caused among the weavers and walkers of the city owing to the neglect of the salutary by-laws of their company, by the master, wardens, and assistants in whom its government is vested. They have, in spite of the reprimands of the judge at the last assize, continued the practice of bringing in non-native workers and housing them in cottages in order to employ them instead of their own workmen. They now pay these 'Foreners' so little that they are forced to seek charitable relief in competition with the natives of the town. In spite of the distress and the high prices, application to the magistrates to put into force the laws for the relief of the poor has proved in vain. Nor will they prevent the export of corn. A meeting of the distressed is called for six o'clock in the morning on a day named, in Perry Wood, which lies to the south-east of the city.[3]

---

[1] Luttrell, iii. 91; Wood, iii. 422–3. The surviving records of the special commission which tried the rioters have also been used. They are among the records of the Clerk of Assize for the Western Circuit. P.R.O. Assizes, 5. 13.

[2] The depression in the industry was a long-standing one. Decline was steady throughout the century. *V.C.H. Worcester*, ii. 290–5; Lipson, pp. 305–12.

[3] P.R.O. Assizes, 5. 13.

Riots took place at about the same time in Shrewsbury, where 300 people assembled at the market cross and proclaimed that the carrying of corn out of the nation would breed a famine.[1] There was an attack, too, upon a load of corn being sent to an inhabitant of Wolverhampton, who protested to the bailiffs of the town that it was for his own use as a baker.[2] 'Tumults in every place by the poore', writes Anthony Wood: 'Mealmen inhance the price and millers.'[3] In Dorsetshire there were riots at Lyme and Weymouth.[4]

The result was the setting-up of a special commission of Oyer et Terminer, already mentioned, to inquire into the riots in Worcestershire, Shropshire, and Herefordshire.[5] Wood wrote, on 20 June, that the judges had returned from Worcester, having passed sentence of death on four; two for breaking open farmers' houses and two for murder; but that they had been reprieved for 18 days. This does not appear, however, to have satisfied the government, for on 15 February 1694 the council ordered that the information presented to the board that day concerning 'the great riots and disorders lately committed in and about the City of Worcester and parts adjacent' should be sent to the attorney-general, 'to cause some of the chiefest abettors and promoters thereof to be strictly prosecuted according to law'.[6]

Meanwhile at Oxford there had been similar disturbances on a lesser scale. On Sunday 29 April 1693 'the poore in Oxford by clamoring brought the price of corne from 9s. to 6s. 2d.'. On the following Sunday, 'poore women in Oxon market clamoring again at the price of Corne, pelting millers, mealmen, bakers etc. with stones', the mayor went to the guildhall, sent for and quieted them.[7] Thereafter the summer appears to have been quiet, though a 'notorious riot' reported from Wallingford in July may well have been due to the continuance of high prices.[8]

---

[1] Wood, iii. 241–2; Luttrell, iii. 88.
[2] P.R.O. Assizes 5. 13. The deposition is in the roll for Shropshire.
[3] Wood, iii. 422.
[4] Luttrell, loc. cit.; P.C. 2. 75, pp. 146–7.
[5] Wood, iii. 425.   [6] P.C. 2. 75, p. 345.
[7] Wood, iii. 421–2; V.C.H. Oxford, ii. 199.
[8] C.S.P. Dom., 1693–4, p. 235. It is difficult to tell whether the government were active in this year in attempting to deal with the causes of disturbance.

The harvest of 1693 brought no relief. It was, indeed, with the single exception of 1661, the worst recorded since the reign of Elizabeth,[1] and was followed in England as elsewhere by a series of popular disturbances.[2] In England, as in Scotland, government action was not lacking. On 19 October the council resolved on a proclamation forbidding the export of corn to France and ordering the strict administration of the laws regulating the internal trade in food-stuffs by the licensing system, as well as those for setting the poor to work.[3] The last of these orders was at this date certainly no more than 'a pious hope',[4] and it seems unlikely that the second did much to meet the problem of scarcity. The prohibition of export to France, which had a political as well as an economic motive, was, however, apparently carried into effect with some vigour, and ten days after the issue of the proclamation Luttrell recorded that eight masters of ships had been taken up for contravening its provisions.[5]

The centre of the trouble this year was Northamptonshire. The date of the first disturbance is obscure, but a local historian records the following: 'A Riot, Wheat being 7s. a Bushell, to stop Tranting [a local word for forestalling, &c.]. One Buckby's Waggon of meal was seized, some of the Rioters were whip'd but very gently at the Sessions but Buckby the Trantor hanged himself Aug. 2nd.'[6] Whether the leniency of the authorities or the suicide of their enemy the corn-dealer more encouraged the mob it is impossible to say, but the trouble did not end here. On 26 October Luttrell records further attacks on corn-dealers in Northampton, the wheat seized from their carts being sold

Luttrell wrote (iii. 86) that the justices of the peace had set a price for corn, which, for wheat, was as high already as 56s. This presumably refers to Middlesex. Wood further states in a letter of 20 May: 'orders are sent to all the seaports to prohibit the exportation of corne' . . . 'this is to please the vulgar but false (quaere)' (Wood, iii. 423). I can find no confirmation of this in administrative records.

[1] J. E. T. Rogers, *The First Nine Years of the Bank of England*, 1887, p. 14.

[2] See the references to disorders in France, where the naval blockade was believed to have intensified the distress, in Luttrell, iii, e.g. p. 257.

[3] P.C. 2. 75; pp. 260–1; Crawford, p. 495; Luttrell, iii. 209 and, for Scotland, p. 213.

[4] Marshall, p. 125.   [5] Luttrell, iii. 217.

[6] *Records of the Borough of Northampton*, 1898, ii. 65. The description is from the MS. of Joseph Hall, a series of eight volumes relative to the town, begun in 1785.

at the next market at 5s. the bushel.[1] On 11 November a news-letter stated upon advice from Northampton that the 'mobile' had been unruly there, corn-wagons from which the sacks had been removed having been thrown into the river on several successive market days.[2] As at Oxford earlier in the year, women took a prominent part in these disturbances, great numbers of them coming into the market with knives stuck in their girdles 'to force corn at their own rates'.[3] Other places in Northamptonshire where similar scenes were witnessed were Wellingborough and Daventry, while corn was also seized from the engrossers' wagons in Banbury, Chipping Norton, and Charlbury in Oxfordshire, the mob saying that 'they were resolved to put the law in execution since the magistrates neglected it'.[4]

Finally, to end a dismal year, in December, when wheat stood at 9s. 6d. a bushel, and the poor were reduced to eating turnips,[5] further tumults were reported, this time from Wycombe and Marlow in Buckinghamshire. In January the Northamptonshire magistrates ordered the Assize of Bread to be set up in every market town in the country.[6] In June there was again trouble in Northampton itself, the mob seizing two loads of corn from an inn. The magistrates and the chief townspeople endeavoured to oppose the mob by force, but were overpowered. In the scuffle, which lasted several hours, two were said to have been killed while 'sixty or seventy received broken pates or bruises'.[7] The council sent the usual instructions to the lord-lieutenant of the county, to the mayor of Northampton and the neighbouring justices, as well as to the corresponding authorities of Peterborough, Kettering, and of Stamford in Lincolnshire, where similar disturbances had taken place.[8] On 14 July, Shrews-

---

[1] Luttrell, iii. 213.

[2] Recognizances in the Sessions Roll for Michaelmas 1693 refer to a riot in Northampton, and the overturning of a cart. Indictments refer to riotous assembly and assault, forcible entry, and stealing barley. A man was bound over to keep the peace towards a baker.   [3] C.S.P. Dom., 1693, p. 397.

[4] Ibid.; Wood, iii. 434. In the Northampton Sessions Roll there is a presentment for buying and selling corn contrary to statute.

[5] Wood, iii. 437; T. Tooke, History of Prices, 1838, i. 30; Luttrell, iii. 240.

[6] Northamptonshire County Records, Sessions Minute Books, Jan. 1694.

[7] C.S.P. Dom., Will. & Mar. vi. 262.

[8] P.C. 2. 75, pp. 438–41.

bury, the secretary of state, wrote to the mayor of Northampton, approving of the vigour which had enabled him and those joined with him to suppress the tumults by their own authority.[1]

Shrewsbury, in whose mind the political fortunes of the government were as usual uppermost, was indeed pleased to be able to inform the absent king that the tumults were mere corn-riots of no political significance.[2] The indifference of the upper classes to the sufferings of the poor at this time is well illustrated in the news-letter to the earl of Derwentwater, already quoted in connexion with the rioting at Northampton; for it stated that whereas the mob acted under the pretence that corn was made dear by buying up great quantities and sending it beyond sea, their action was rather 'to satisfy an idle and thievish humour the mob was at present possessed withal out of which they must be well whipped'.[3]

In the following years—years of great political excitement—the mob, except in London, was quieter. The average price of wheat in 1695 fell considerably, and there was little activity on the part of the government. Luttrell recorded on 22 August that the lords justices, considering the unseasonableness of the weather, had for the present prohibited the exportation of corn, but strangely enough the minutes of the proceedings of lords justices for this period, calendared among the State Papers, show no trace of such action, nor does there appear to be any extant proclamation to this effect.[4] Only in December was the council informed by the petitions of the inhabitants of various parishes on either side of the Suffolk–Essex borders of serious attacks upon corn-wagons. The usual directions to the local justices followed, and upon the receipt of their

[1] *C.S.P. Dom.*, *1694–5*, p. 227.

[2] Coxe, *Shrewsbury Correspondence*, 1821, pp. 52–4.

[3] *C.S.P. Dom.*, *1696*, p. 262. The meagre information obtainable from the Sessions Records about the Northamptonshire riots—there is none for 1694—is, no doubt, due to the trials of the chief offenders having taken place at the assizes. The town clerk of Northampton informs me that the chamberlain's accounts for October 1693 include a payment to a Mr. Lee for business at the assizes about the riot. There are no assize records of this period for this circuit.

[4] Luttrell, iii. 515.

report in the following February the attorney-general was instructed to proceed against the offenders.[1]

The average price of wheat for 1696 was the highest recorded for the whole period.[2] The question of the food supply receives, however, no mention in the records of the central government, and the riots which took place in the summer of that year can be traced directly to the shortage of coin, and will be treated of in that connexion.

Similarly in 1697, when prices fell a little, the disturbances among the weavers of London and elsewhere, and the nail-makers of Warwickshire, though no doubt connected with the dearness of food, produce no explicit reference to prices, nor is there evidence of any government action for their control.[3] What effect precisely the evidence of popular discontent had on the decision to make peace it is difficult to ascertain. Yet it is interesting to find Shrewsbury, in the previous August, advocating the speedy initiation of peace proposals, writing to the king: 'the circumstances here are different from those of any country: suffering makes men dissatisfied; and how far that, by degrees, may be improved to the ruin of the whole, nobody can tell'.[4]

Certainly, the respite given to the government by the peace was of short duration, for after the inordinately wet summer of 1698, yet another deficient harvest made the food problem once more acute.[5] In Scotland, where the extreme scarcity caused large numbers of the inhabitants to cross the border in search of food, and on the Continent, there was a serious shortage of corn.[6] In October the Dutch prohibited under serious penalties the exporting or the engrossing of corn, and also its distillation for spirits.[7]

The first move of the government in England was a

---

[1] P.C. 2. 76, pp. 230 and 287. There had been corn-riots in Suffolk as early as October. S. and B. Webb, *The Parish and the County*, 1906, p. 488, n.

[2] Certain prisoners in the Buckinghamshire county jail petitioned for an allowance of 3*d.* a day for bread, 'setting out that their whole subsistence depended upon the said allowance of bread, and that the prices of wheat still continued very high'. *Buckingham County Records*, ii. 86.

[3] For these disturbances see *infra*, Chap. IV.

[4] Coxe, p. 136.

[5] Tooke, p. 31.

[6] *C.S.P. Dom., 1698*, ix. 409 and 425.

[7] Luttrell, iv. 439.

proclamation for enforcing the laws against engrossing and for setting the poor to work, since it was stated: 'The prices of corn do already exceed the rates in the said Act of King Charles the Second [15 Car. II, cap. 7] and is [sic] likely to grow much dearer to the great oppression of the poor, in part because the said Acts are not duly put in execution.'[1] Luttrell notes, presumably with surprise, that the proclamation made no mention of export.[2]

Nevertheless, although no actual disorder is recorded, the action taken was felt to be insufficient, and the difficulties of London were brought home in a petition from the justices and grand jury of Middlesex against excessive distillation.[3] Parliament was therefore occupied between January and March 1699 in discussing bills dealing with exportation and excessive distillation.[4] Export was prohibited first till the following February and then until September of that year, 1700,[5] while excessive distilling was likewise prohibited.[6]

Whether or not this legislative activity was responsible for ameliorating the position, these years show little signs of popular turbulence, with the exception of one attack upon a corn-dealer's stores which took place at Truro in March 1700,[7] and of a mysterious affair at Nottingham, apparently in 1701, when an alderman appeased the riotous mob by distributing an unwilling dealer's corn.[8] Thereafter prices began to drop, and the next seven years are years of low prices with the exception of 1704, which followed a bad harvest.[9] Thus even large exports of corn such as Luttrell records as made to Holland between 1700 and 1702 produced no outbreak of discontent.[10]

[1] P.C. 2. 77, pp. 249–51; C.S.P. Dom., 1698, p. 402.
[2] Luttrell, iv. 438.   [3] Dowdell, p. 168.
[4] Luttrell, iv. 463–89, passim. Throughout the year both houses discussed bills for the relief of the poor. Ibid.
[5] Stats. of Realm, 10 Will. III, cap. 3, and 11 Will. III, cap. 1.
[6] Ibid., 10 Will. III, cap. 4.   [7] P.C. 2. 77, p. 439.
[8] Nottingham Borough Records, v. 405. At midsummer 1700, the bread allowance to the Buckinghamshire prisoners was reduced to 2½d. Buckingham County Records, ii. 259.   [9] Tooke, i. 35.
[10] Luttrell, v, passim. In 1700 a Hertfordshire deposition made by one Richard Harwood of Ware, mealman, included the statement that wheat was very cheap 'by reason no London loaders came down'. Hertford County Records, ii. 24. For the general prosperity prevailing at the turn of the century, see A. Andréadès, History of the Bank of England, p. 114.

Not until 1708 do we reach the last food crisis of the period, which, lasting well into 1710, coincided with important political events. This, no doubt, explains in part the popular violence with which these events were accompanied, as also the growth of a determined peace party.

In September 1708 Lady Pye wrote to Abigail Harley from Derby: 'We had an unkindly spring and now an uncomfortable wet autumn, but worst for harvest. All grades much risen.'[1] The steepness of the rise in prices was indeed sharper in these years than at any other time in the period under discussion. From 27s. 3d. at which wheat stood on Lady Day 1708 it rose to 46s. 3d. by Michaelmas, to 57s. 6d. by Lady Day 1709, and to 81s. 9d. by Michaelmas, a price at which it still stood on Lady Day 1710.[2]

The populace was not slow to react. In May 1709 it was reported from Essex that mobs of women amounting to hundreds were on the move and had threatened to 'fire divers houses, and shoot several persons, by reason they have been dealers in corn to London, on pretence they make the same dear'. In the same month the mayor of Bristol wrote to Sunderland, the secretary of state, that four hundred people, the notorious colliers of Kingswood forest, were advancing upon the city under pretence of demanding bread and committing great disorders. They in fact entered the city and caused a great deal of trouble before the magistrates succeeded in appeasing them by selling them corn at below the ordinary rate.[3] The harvest of that year brought, as we have seen, no relief, and Luttrell recorded under the date 1 October that in the previous week a corn-factor employed in buying up wheat for export at Kingston market was almost mobbed, together with some foreigners who were with him.[4] Northamptonshire as usual provided its quota of disorder.[5]

---

[1] H.M.C. Portland, iv. 504.

[2] Tooke, i. 36. Holland was similarly affected. A. Boyer, Annals of Queen Anne, Eighth Year, pp. 2–3.

[3] J. Latimer, Annals of Bristol in the Eighteenth Century, pp. 78–9; H.M.C. Rep. VIII, app. 1, sec. 1, Papers of the Duke of Marlborough, p. 46; W. Barrett, History of the City of Bristol, p. 696. Coggeshall, one of the places mentioned in connexion with the Essex riots, had been the scene of a short-lived wool-combers' union in 1688–90. This may be another case of industrial discontent venting itself in a corn-riot. Lipson, iii. 397–8.   [4] Luttrell, vi. 494.

[5] The Northamptonshire Sessions Roll for 1710 contains recognizances referring

London itself, with coastal shipping disorganized by the war, appears to have felt the scarcity most keenly of all. And for once we find great activity on the part of the local authorities. For this activity the constant intervention of the central government must be held at least in part responsible.[1]

On 28 September the council summoned the justices of Middlesex to attend it, to consider the regulation of the price of corn. They were informed by Lord Somers, the lord president, that although they could not interfere with exports without an act of parliament, yet they could and should prevent regrating and forestalling.[2] The existence of such practices in the city was denied by the lord mayor in a letter to Sunderland. He suggested, on the contrary, that the high prices were due to export and proposed that the government should provide a convoy to enable corn to be shipped from the north, where it was selling for 40s.[3] The justices of Middlesex and Westminster made an inquiry into the question, and at their Michaelmas sessions issued an order that current market prices should be adhered to. In a further representation to the council in October, they stressed the evil effects of market manipulation and suggested renewing the regulation of the price of bread under the act of Henry VIII.[4] By an act passed later on in the winter, the old Assize of Bread was indeed revived.[5]

Evidence that some, at least, of this activity was more than a mere formality is shown by the fact that on 6 October Luttrell records an order to the attorney-general, 'to prosecute several corn factors, mealmen and others, in the county of Middlesex, for engrossing corn upon market days in the towns of the said county'.[6] On 24 October the government attempted to extend these activities by a proclamation for the execution of the forestalling laws.[7]

to stopping corn-wagons and riotously removing their contents. It is possible that enclosures in Northamptonshire caused a drift of population to the towns which the new woollen manufactures may have failed wholly to absorb. J. Morton, *Natural History of Northamptonshire*, 1712, p. 15.

1 Dowdell, p. 169.   2 Luttrell, vi, loc. cit.
3 Sharpe, ii. 631.   4 Boyer, pp. 199–200.
5 Luttrell, vi. 496; Stats. of Realm, 8 Anne, cap. 19.
6 Luttrell, vi. 496.   7 Crawford, p. 530; Luttrell, vi. 503.

As usual, scarcity abroad coincided with, and threatened to intensify, that at home, and the queen's speech on 15 November earnestly recommended the redressing of excessive exportation for the sake of the poor. Two days later the Commons took into consideration that part of the queen's speech and resolved that an address should be made requesting an immediate embargo on all corn-ships, and ordered a bill to be brought in to prevent exportation for nine months.[1] This bill received the royal assent on 10 December, and was apparently sufficient for the crisis to pass with no further outbreaks.[2]

Nevertheless, even a decided drop in prices was not sufficient to ensure safety for corn-dealers, and in December 1712 we find Sir John Lambert praying the queen's protection for some corn bought in Hampshire, and stored in warehouses at Redbridge, near Southampton. The life of his factor had been threatened in a letter in a large illiterate hand which survives among the documents of the case, and the warehouses had actually been beseiged by a mob for several days, apparently with the full approval of even the more substantial inhabitants of Romsey. The unwillingness of the local justices to take action may also indicate the strong local feeling against such exportation.[3]

From the nature of the available sources, it is impossible accurately to enumerate the disturbances arising in this period over the question of the food supply. If an Anthony Wood, for instance, had existed in any other county town, we might be in a position to chronicle there disturbances similar to those at Oxford. And many such may now be concealed by a curt indictment for riotous assembly or assault in surviving quarter-sessions records. From the records which are available it is nevertheless possible to draw certain general conclusions which may be upheld with some certainty.

In spite, then, of the close connexion in the popular mind

---

[1] Luttrell, vi. 511–12.

[2] Ibid., vi. 513–21; Stats. of Realm, 8 Anne, cap. 2. Some idea of the lack of clear policy can be gained from the fact that in Jan. 1710, when the scarcity was at its height, the council ordered the duke of Newcastle, as Custos Rotulorum of the East Riding of Yorkshire, to take steps for the taxation of imported corn. *H.M.C. Portland*, ii. 210.   [3] State Papers, Anne, bundle 37.

between corn exports and scarcity at home, it does not appear that the system of bounties was of major importance in this period, since, with the exception of isolated instances in 1700 and 1712, the years of disturbances were all years in which corn prices much exceeded those at which the bounty was payable. Indeed, it does not appear to have been until after 1715 that the export of corn from England became at all considerable. As far as can be seen it exceeded 100,000 quarters only in 1675–8, 1703, 1706, and 1707, of the years before 1711, although averaging 170,000 quarters in the next four years.[1] The total restriction placed on export by the government in 1699 and 1709 may thus be taken rather as earnest of good intentions than as a positive contribution to the problem of scarcity,[2] and a similar remark might well be made about the six months' suspension of the bounty in 1700.[3]

Nor, in this period, does the excessive distillation of spirits play a part in raising prices comparable to that which it did after 1714. This was true in spite of the impetus given to home-produced liquors by the embargo upon French brandies. The problem was, however, already serious enough to call for legislative action in 1699, when an act against excessive distilling was passed to meet the probability of excessive exports due to similar restriction elsewhere,[4] and probably no reluctance was shown in granting, in March of the same year, a patent to one Abraham Bayly, Esq., and four other gentlemen for the invention of 'drawing low wines and spirits from turnips, carrots and parsnips', which, it was claimed, would make a great saving in the consumption of corn.[5] Similarly, the use in the making of starch of 'wholesome corn grown in the realm' had been prohibited by a proclamation of August 1661.[6]

In view of the smallness of the numbers of troops actually drawn from and supplied from England, engaged in the wars

[1] Gras, pp. 113–14 and 418–19. This compares with an annual average export of over 300,000 quarters in the years 1731–9. Barnes, p. 15.

[2] Stats. of Realm, 10 Will. III, cap. 3, and 8 Anne, cap. 2.

[3] Ibid., 11 Will. III, cap. 1.

[4] Ibid., 10 Will. III, cap. 4. There had been a petition about it from Bristol. Latimer, p. 488.

[5] *C.S.P. Dom., 1699–1700*, p. 89.   [6] Ibid., *1661–2*, p. 58.

of the period, one may agree to doubt that they played any considerable part in raising prices, though a growth of exports was noted during the third Dutch war. In a letter of 1672 indeed we find the war mentioned as having a depressing effect on prices. This was due no doubt to its effect on shipping.[1]

One must conclude, therefore, with Tooke, that, in an age of restricted markets, the climatic accidents productive of good and bad harvest were the prime cause of the enormous fluctuations in corn prices, and hence of the outbreaks of discontent in these years.[2] The 'seven lean years' of the last decade of the century can easily be explained in this way. And in considering them and their effects it should be remembered that, while the figures themselves are vivid enough, it is probable that the real rise from the consumers' point of view is hidden by the depressive effect on money prices of the acute shortage of coin during the recoinage.[3]

It is not hard to see how much the effect of climatic changes was intensified by the peculiar conditions of inland transport prevailing during this period. Means of inland transport being so deficient, local surpluses when they existed would of necessity tend to be exported overseas, especially since, in view of the fact that western Europe is largely a climatic unit, high prices would probably be found to exist over the whole area at once. In December 1698, for instance, Ellis, the under-secretary of state, wrote to the English ambassador at The Hague that the elector of Bavaria had sent an agent to solicit permission to transport a quantity of corn to Flanders, and that it was not doubted but that he would obtain leave, there being plenty of corn in the west in spite of the acute scarcity in the north.[4]

The only large inland area which was in any sense unified was that which supplied the rapidly growing needs of London, that is to say, the eastern and southern counties and the upper Thames valley.[5] Further unification was pre-

---

[1] Barnes, p. 13; *C.S.P. Dom., 1671–2*, pp. 235–6.
[2] Tooke, i, pt. i.
[3] For the recoinage measures and their social effects see *infra*, Chap. V.
[4] *C.S.P. Dom., 1698*, p. 425; Gras, *passim*.
[5] Barnes, pp. 11–12. But even so fluctuations outside the metropolis itself were greater than those within it. Gilboy, pp. 55–6. River transport made supplies easy to certain other towns, e.g. Nottingham. Chambers, p. 87.

vented not only by difficulties of transport, but by government action deliberately restraining, as forestalling, regrating, and engrossing, the activities of inland corn-traders.[1] The revival of medieval legislation against the internal corn trade was indeed a feature of every high-price period until the inadequacy of such measures to meet new conditions became finally apparent in the crisis of 1766.[2] There was then, in government policy, a contradiction between the persistence of the medieval provision policy in the internal regulation of trade, which even went as far as attempting to enforce price-fixing by the local authorities, and its abandonment, at least in theory, in the sphere of foreign trade.[3]

To this charge the government of the period could undoubtedly have replied that public opinion, such as it was, supported it. The landowners were convinced that the destruction of the tiny enclosed markets which were their preserves would ruin them. Thus early canal-building and river-navigation schemes which threatened their virtual monopolies met from them, and from towns particularly favoured by existing waterways, uncompromising resistance.[4] In 1699, for instance, Derbyshire landowners objected, with apparent success, to the River Derwent Navigation Bill on the ground that it would enable Derby traders to determine corn prices.[5]

More important from our point of view is the intensely hostile feeling of the common people to the internal, as well as the export, trade in corn. Attacks on corn-dealers, and on dealers in more perishable food-stuffs, whose wares cannot have been meant for long journeys, are perhaps the most characteristic of the popular disturbances which we have chronicled. The significance of this can be seen by a glance at the map at the end of this work. Mr. D. G.

---

[1] Municipal action in this direction was also occasionally forthcoming, e.g. in Nottingham, in June 1699. *Nottingham Borough Records*, v. 400–1.
[2] Barnes, pp. 38–45.   [3] Heckscher, ii. 97.
[4] T. S. Willan, *River Navigation in England*, 1936, p. 46.
[5] *H.M.C. Cowper*, pp. 383–4. The Nottingham corporation also opposed the bill. They opposed, too, a River Trent Navigation Bill on the ground that it would 'Ingrosse the Navigation and Monopolize Trade between 2 or 3 persons to the prejudice of the country in general and this town in particular'. Opposition to a bill for making the Avon navigable to Bath was strengthened by the millers who used it for water-power. Latimer, *Annals of Bristol in the Seventeenth Century*, p. 484.

Barnes, dealing with the riots of the middle of the eighteenth century, when large-scale export aroused the old fears of starvation, observes that 'such fears were generally stronger in the northern and western districts of the country than in the wheat districts on the east and south coast'.[1] On the other hand, the riots we have dealt with appear to be either in the south-midland or East Anglian corn districts, whence London drew its supplies, or in the ports of Hampshire, Dorset, and Cornwall. In the poverty-stricken north, apart from disturbances directly traceable to the effects of the recoinage, there appears to have been no trouble.

The type of area in which the disorders took place, and the preoccupation of the authorities, central and local, with the activities of the political and religious opposition groups, explain certain features of the period, otherwise perplexing. There was, for instance, no revival of the old practice of the buying and storing of grain by municipal or county authorities. In this respect, both in Ireland in 1667 and in Scotland, where the famine years at the end of the century were even more severely felt, the authorities did act.[2] In England such measures were not even suggested.

The chief defect in the economic organization of the country from the point of view of the food supply, the restriction of markets, was only intensified by the spasmodic campaigns against the inland trade. The old laws against forestalling and engrossing bore little relation to the economic theory or the economic practice of the new age. Had the disorders been still more severe they might well have ousted assassination plots and rumours of invasion from the first place in the interests of successive secretaries of state. As it was they served only to intensify the growing belief among the upper classes that idleness rather than genuine poverty was the real cause of distress, and that high prices were needed to make the poor work hard enough to maintain the productive capacity of the country.[3]

Just as it was the problem of a rapidly rising poor-rate which forced the social problem into prominence at the end of the eighteenth century, so this same problem drew atten-

---

[1] Barnes, p. 32. [2] *C.S.P. Dom.*, *1666–7*, p. 582, and *1698*, p. 425.
[2] Furniss, *passim* and especially the quotation from John Law on p. 22.

tion to it at an earlier period. Commenting on the high prices prevailing in January 1710, a Buckinghamshire correspondent of Ralph Verney's wrote, ''tis very hard with poor people and they are ready to famish and so many sessions have been harping on it, I marvell no Act passes about erecting workhouses; or for the better employing so many hands for the good of the Kingdom. Otherwise the nation must sink under the burthen and the parishes will hardly be able to keep 'em.'[1]

Thus the class which both controlled local government and influenced most profoundly through parliament the policies of the administration, while not wholly unconcerned about the problem of poverty, regarded it from a very special standpoint. The technique of economic thinking long employed in dealing with complicated questions of the exchanges and the balance of trade was scarcely utilized for the better comprehension of internal maladjustments in the economic system. Those who were concerned with it did not think of the question as one of prices and wages. Out of the various sections of the population who were suffering from the economic changes of the day it was the unemployed alone whose situation seemed to call for intervention. And the only type of intervention which could be conceived was one which involved their direct employment by the state in some form of self-supporting or profit-making enterprise. This conception, whatever its economic merits, was scarcely feasible in an age when the whole art of social administration had still to be learnt.

The afflicted classes themselves varied in temper between a condition of mute resignation, in face of the uncomprehended hardships of their lot, and one of sullen antagonism against those apparently responsible for them. Their resentment, when unemployment and high prices combined to make conditions unendurable, vented itself in attacks upon corn-dealers and millers—attacks which often must have degenerated into mere excuses for crime. Among the plunder of the Worcestershire rioters in 1693 were not merely sacks of grain, but 25s. 2d. in money and 'three cloth coats valor triginti solidi'.[2]

[1] *Verney Letters*, i. 278.

[2] P.R.O. Assizes, 5. 13.

IV

AGRICULTURE AND INDUSTRY

THE problem of enclosures, which had been for two centuries the main cause of agrarian discontent, plays little direct part in the history of disorder in this period. Recent opinion holds this fact to be due not so much to the slowing-down of the enclosing movement as to a change in public opinion, and to the emergence of new outlets for the displaced population.[1]

There are isolated local instances of attacks on enclosures, but where there is sufficient detail available to make the matter clear it would appear that they were directed for the most part against park enclosures made for sport or pleasure rather than against enclosures for pasture or tillage, and may thus be viewed as an extension of the activities of poachers.[2]

There appears to be no evidence of an outburst of agrarian crime to justify the act of 1670 against the destruction of enclosures, rick-firing, and cattle-maiming.[3]

Other attacks may have been due merely to dislike of an unpopular neighbour or landlord. In May 1689 Mrs. Marbury, of Marbury, in Cheshire, employed two men to watch by night over a fence constructed by her—a precaution which proved insufficient.[4]

Sometimes the dispute over rights of common might be longstanding. The enclosures made by Anthony Townshend at Chilesmore led to rioting in March 1666 by the citizens of the neighbouring town of Coventry. They were covertly encouraged by the magistrates of the city, who were in consequence threatened with the loss of their charter. Although an agreement was arrived at on this occasion, there was even more serious rioting there in January 1689, when

---

[1] Lipson, ii. 407–19.

[2] *Surrey County Records*, ed. Jenkinson, 35, 1934, p. 130; *C.S.P. Dom., 1663–4*, p. 219; *1701–2*, p. 43; Crawford, p. 505; *Hertford County Records*, ii. 3.

[3] Stats. of Realm, 22 & 23 Car. II, cap. 7. For a projected statute against the destruction of enclosures see a paper of 1698. *H.M.C. Portland*, viii. 51.

[4] Cheshire County Records, Sessions Roll of July 1689.

many of the burgesses of the city, 'with a great Rabble of Dissolute people', destroyed his fences and ditches, threatened to fire his house, and so forced him to abandon it to them, and at the time of his petition to the council two months later were stocking his grounds 'with their own cattle in defiance of all law and right'.[1]

Even more unpleasant were the experiences of Nathaniel Reading, Esq., as described in his petition of 3 June 1697. On 15 April in that year 'divers lewd persons' set fire to his house at Santoft in the manor of Epworth in Lincolnshire. At midnight on 24 May ten men in disguise discharged guns at some servants he had in another house, threatened to kill them, and destroyed that house also. On the following night they made 'several Fires about his fences, and several Damms and Dykes made for the preservation of his corne', and destroyed a quantity of building material. On 24 June he reported to the council that since the issue of an order offering a free pardon and reward for the discovery of the offenders, he had suffered 'further great outrages'. The attorney-general was thereupon ordered to inquire into the matter. The place, date, and mention of dams and dikes suggests that this affair may have been connected with the disorders among the inhabitants of the fens, to which we shall refer shortly.[2]

The one clear case of an enclosure riot comes from the very end of the period. On 24 May 1710 the duke of Shrewsbury, then lord chamberlain, was approached with an account of riots in Northamptonshire due to enclosures by William, second marquis of Powis. The petitioner, Mr. Charles Kirkham, said that there was 'no refuge now but the benefit of her Majesty's gracious proclamation'. A week later a Capt. J. Wroth reported from Oundle that, acting upon instructions to prevent any riots during the holidays at Benefield, in Northamptonshire, he had marched there on the previous day. He declared that the greatest part of the gentry thought Lord Powis's enclosure a great injustice to the poor. Even making allowance for the local gentry's fear of rioting, the mention of an injustice to the poor by members

[1] P.C. 2. 58, pp. 404, 410, 414; ibid. 2. 59, pp. 22 and 55–6; ibid. 2. 73, p. 30.
[2] Ibid. 2. 77, pp. 25 and 31.

of the landed classes at that time suggests that it must have been particularly flagrant.[1]

In 1671 the enclosures made by the duchess of Cleveland in the Forest of Dean were violently destroyed. This did not prevent her receiving another grant of ironworks there two years later.[2]

The destruction of illegal enclosures also caused rioting. On this occasion it was not great landlords but the colliers of Kingswood who were guilty, they having built cottages in the forest area which they were forcibly required to evacuate when the mining operations came to an end.[3]

Other rural disturbances were due to some specific wrong. The inhabitants of the isle of Portland were granted in 1665 their old rights of payment for the stone quarried from their commons. These were neglected, apparently, when stone was quarried for the rebuilding of St. Paul's in 1678, and there were riots in consequence.[4]

Even the necessary improvements in the facilities for inland navigation might lead to rioting when a local interest was threatened. In 1669 the works of the New River company at Ware were demolished on the grounds that they would prejudice the navigation of Ware and Hertford.[5]

Finally, one may note that the destruction by government order of English tobacco-plantations in the interest of the American colonies caused rioting in Gloucestershire.[6]

If the riots of the fenmen were on the largest scale of any of the rural disturbances of the period, their grievances were the most understandable. The effect of the drainage schemes was to abolish the haunts of fish and wild-fowl,

[1] S.P. Anne, 12, no. 81. It is not clear what proclamation is referred to. There is no mention of the riot in the Quarter Sessions Records. Lord Powis did not long enjoy his ill-gotten gains, as in 1724 he sold the manor, together with other properties in the county. *V.C.H. Northampton*, iii. 79. Landholding and common-rights were particularly widely diffused in this then corn-growing county, and there had been strenuous resistance to the enclosures of James I's reign. Slater, p. 197; E. M. Leonard, 'Enclosure of the Common Fields in the Seventeenth Century', *T.R.H.S.* N.S. xiv, 1905.

[2] P.C. 2. 63, p. 123; C. H. Hartmann, *Clifford of the Cabal*, 1937, pp. 274–5.

[3] P.C. 2. 62, p. 284; *C.S.P. Dom., 1670*, pp. 435–6.

[4] Ibid., *1665–6*, pp. 12–13; P.C. 2. 66, p. 292.

[5] Ibid. 2. 62, pp. 45–9, 67, 77, 81, and 138.

[6] *C.S.P. Dom., 1662–3*, p. 602.

their main source of livelihood, and their rights of common on the existing patches of terra firma were too often ignored.[1]

There had been serious riots in the first half of the century and the Civil War had seen widespread destruction of the obnoxious draining works. When work was restarted, trouble followed almost at once. There was rioting in Hatfield Chase in July 1661, and at Wildmore Fen in Lincolnshire in August 1663.[2] In 1667 there was rioting in Peterborough Great Fen and in 1669 at Mildenhall in Suffolk.[3] In Bedford Level it had been found necessary to issue a proclamation against rioting in 1662. The drainage act of 1663 therefore provided recompense for persons through whose grounds the works cut, but ignored the claims of fishermen and fowlers. Any who interfered with the drainage works were to pay treble damages. Penalties were also to be enforced against owners of common rights who should disturb any improvements or enclosures after an arrangement for dividing and enclosing the commons had been arrived at.[4]

The most serious trouble in this period took place in 1699 when about 1,100 men were reported to have destroyed the drainage works in Deeping Fen in Lincolnshire, as well as a number of houses, barns, and mills, and to be threatening further mischief. On 19 January the council instructed the high sheriff and justices of Lincolnshire to put into effect the laws against rioting and especially the statute 13 Henry IV, cap. 7, 'for taking the power of the County upon such occasions'. The earl of Lindsey, lord-lieutenant of the county, was ordered to assist them.[5] The trouble was not, however, to be thus easily checked. In March the Company of Conservators of Bedford Level asked the council for protection, they having received notice of a design for destroying their drainage works. They referred to the recent destruction of the Deeping Fen works 'under colour and pretence of Football playing'. Now there was to be a game of football and other sports to take place on Coats' Green by Whittelsea

[1] Darby, chap. xii; Ernle, p. 118; Chambers, pp. 193–5.

[2] P.C. 2. 55, pp. 299, 515–17, 546, 558, 588, 612, 633, 646, 657; *C.S.P. Dom.*, *1663–4*, p. 160; *1664–5*, p. 126.

[3] P.C. 2. 59, pp. 430, 439, 463, 475; 61, pp. 311, 325, 356, 358.

[4] P.C. 2. 55, p. 38; Stats. of Realm, 15 Car. II, cap. 17.

[5] P.C. 2. 77, p. 293.

on or about the 14th of March. Notice of this had been given by a paper affixed on March bridge, which suggests an unexpectedly high standard of literacy among the poorest classes of a backward area. Further, several persons had been heard to say that the captain of the mob which had committed the riot in Deeping Fen would be there to lead the mob in their design upon the Bedford Level works. The council exhorted the sheriff and justices of Norfolk to prevent unlawful assemblies, and showed their fear of the possible spreading of the disorders by sending similar instructions to the authorities of the Isle of Ely, of Cambridgeshire, Huntingdonshire, and Northamptonshire.[1]

The silence of the records leads one to believe these measures to have been successful, but in June trouble was again reported from Lincolnshire, where the inhabitants of Croyland had driven their cattle into the lands claimed by the Deeping Fen company, had erected booths upon them, and set up a guard over the cattle to prevent any action by the company's servants.[2] The justices and the lord-lieutenant were in the usual form ordered to see to the suppression of the riot. In July, Lord Raby was appointed head of a commission to inquire into the riots in Lincolnshire which had resulted in submerging many thousands of acres under the sea.[3]

Still the fenmen were not quieted. In May 1701 the council again sent letters to the county authorities urging them to take precautions, since a design for destroying the drainage works had been discovered to be in contemplation for the next holidays and its promoters had 'dispersed papers of Verses Inviteing great numbers of like Disorderly Persons to their Assistance therein'.[4]

'It was not', writes Lord Ernle, 'till after 1714 that the riots caused by the reclamations ceased to disturb the peace of the country. By that time the object was partially achieved and many of the swamps and marshes of the fen districts were restored to the ague-shivering, fever-stricken inhabitants in their primitive unproductiveness.'[5]

The fact that there were as yet few places in which there

[1] P.C. 2. 77, p. 309.   [2] Ibid., pp. 350–1.
[3] *Wentworth Papers*, introduction, p. 7.   [4] P.C. 2. 78, p. 208.
[5] Ernle, p. 119.

were to be found concentrated large numbers of workers engaged in a particular industry may explain why industrial disturbances do not figure largely in the history of this period. But it must be remembered that much work remains to be done in this field and that our knowledge of its economic organization is by no means complete. One may, perhaps, lay down the general rule that the so-called 'domestic system', while not free from gross exploitation, did little to bring the workers together in a way which might enable them to combine for common action. Even so, numerous exceptions fall to be chronicled here.

The great woollen-weaving industry naturally attracts one's interest first. There was discontent, which we have already noted in the case of Worcester, at the neglect of the old laws governing admission to the industry. To this may perhaps be traced the riots at Colchester in August 1675.[1] In June 1696 there were fears of disturbance among the weavers of Norwich owing to the prevalence of unemployment there.[2]

Efforts were made to bring the old laws into force. In May 1699, for instance, the mayor, burgesses, and inhabitants of Wilton and places adjacent engaged in the 'art or mystery of clothing and weaving' petitioned for power to make by-laws in order to prevent people coming into the trade without apprenticeship.[3] Similar causes were probably responsible for the trouble among the weavers, combers, and other workers in the woollen industry reported from Taunton, Tiverton, and Bristol in March 1707.[4]

The other preponderant fear was that of foreign competition. It was believed that this could be rendered less dangerous if weavers were prevented from going abroad or exporting their machines. The rumour that weavers from Exeter were going to France and Ireland and that fulling-mills were being taken caused rioting at Exeter and Topsham in the autumn of 1675.[5]

---

[1] C.S.P. Dom., 1675–6, pp. 352 and 513; P.C. 2. 65, pp. 17 and 20.
[2] C.S.P. Dom., 1696, pp. 247–8.
[3] C.S.P. Dom., 1699–1700, p. 178.
[4] Lipson, iii. 392–5; H.M.C. Portland, iv. 393.
[5] C.S.P. Dom., 1675–6, p. 329; P.C. 2. 65, p. 6. There appears to have been no riot within this period as serious as that at Tiverton in 1720 against the importation into the town of Irish worsted to be dyed in the piece. Dunsford, *Historical Memoirs of Tiverton*, ed. of 1836, pp. 52–3.

Trouble also arose out of an act of 1662 which gave the master weavers of Norwich and other places in Norfolk and Suffolk the right to search for, seize, and exact fines for defective yarn in the possession of wool-combers. The latter complained in 1693 that the weavers had abused their powers in order to plunder them and their houses. They added a pleasing historical touch to the recital of their grievances by comparing the exactions of the weavers to those of Empson and Dudley.[1]

In London the chief source of trouble was to be found among the silk-weavers. Their trade was hit by imports from France, by the work of French weavers who had settled among them, and, most severely of all, as time went on by imports from the East. If we add to this the fact that not only their apprentices but the weavers themselves were suspected of holding political opinions hostile to the régime, one can understand the alarm with which manifestations of discontent among them were viewed. In August 1664 a letter to Bennet, the secretary of state, spoke of riotous meetings in Moorfields of butchers and weavers under pretence of wrestling. 'Most of the weavers', continued his correspondent, 'are fanatics; they are forty thousand able men and very few well affected. They made another uproar last night which troubled honest people, as that was their old method before the late wars.'[2]

Their first considerable outburst seems, however, to be traceable to a strictly economic cause of discontent, namely the introduction of the engine-loom, which was expected to cause great unemployment. There was rioting for several days in London, Westminster, Southwark, and the neighbourhood. Not only were the offending machines destroyed but the French weavers were attacked and their looms burnt. It seems, indeed, according to one account, that it was against them that the riots were in the first instance exclusively directed.[3] One of the directors of the East India Company

[1] Stats. of Realm, 14 Car. II, cap. 5; *C.J.* xi. 22 and 95; *C.S.P. Dom., 1701–2*, p. 579; Lipson, ii. 48.   [2] *C.S.P. Dom., 1663–4*, p. 664.

[3] P.C. 2. 64, pp. 490–1; *C.S.P. Dom., 1675–6*, pp. 250–63, 475–6; *Middlesex County Records*, ed. Jeaffreson, 1892, iv. 61–5; *Hatton Correspondence*, i. 120; *H.M.C. le Fleming*, pp. 124–5; A. P. Wadsworth and J. de L. Mann, *The Cotton Trade and Industrial Lancashire*, 1931, p. 101.

was thanked for his share in restoring order, so it is possible
that some of the rioters' animosity was directed against the
Company and its property.[1]

It has been recently asserted that between 1675 and the
prosecution of a weaver in 1729 for 'mutiny', and for partici-
pating in an unlawful assembly of weavers, there were no
disturbances among them.[2] This is a totally inaccurate
picture of the situation.

In the summer of 1683 so great was the distress among
them that the Rye House plotters considered that they could
get five thousand of them to rise at an hour's warning if
they could find money to pay them.[3] In August there was
the fear of a rising of the weavers' apprentices against the
French if their petition against them was ignored. The
train-bands were kept out, and it was suggested that a company of horse should be quartered in Whitechapel.[4]

It was, however, in the tumultuous petitioning of parliament that the authorities saw most cause for alarm. They
could not, like the Speaker of the house of commons, referring to the statute against it of 1661, 'well forget the
Method how our late Miseries, like the Waves of the Sea
came in upon us. First, the People were invited to petition
to give colour to some illegal demands, then they must
remonstrate, then they must protest, then they must cove-
nant, then they must associate, then they must engage
against our lawful Government and for the maintenance of
the most horrid tyranny that ever was invented.'[5]

From the beginning, the government set up by the
Revolution was determined to prevent the practice.[6] When,
in 1689, the officers of the silk-weavers' companies of
London and Canterbury asked to be heard, before the bill
enjoining the wearing of woollens was voted on by the Lords,
they were accompanied by a mob of silk-weavers amounting,
according to one observer, to above 20,000 in number.
The House was guarded by its own order with two companies
of the horse-bands, and by the constables of Westminster

---

[1] *Court Minutes of the East India Company, 1674–6*, p. 204.
[2] Dowdell, p. 155.   [3] *C.S.P. Dom., 1683* (1), p. 383.
[4] Ibid. (2), p. 330.
[5] Stats. of Realm, 13 Car. II, cap. 5; *L.J.* xi. 329–30.
[6] Lord Mayor's Proclamation, Feb. 1689; Luttrell, i. 499.

with their beadles. Its members took advantage of the suggestion that political discontent was behind the agitation to ask the king for some of the horse and foot guards to aid the civil power. It does not appear whether this request was acceded to, but the lord mayor ordered a regiment of militia to be on guard in London, and the lord-lieutenant of the Tower ordered out several companies in the Hamlets. Finally, the sheriff of Middlesex was commanded to be in readiness with the posse and constables, and the deputy lieutenants and justices of the peace of the county were instructed to be vigilant in preserving the peace. Although these preparations sufficed to overcome the mob and to enable the Lords to dispense with the train-bands, who had been posted in Palace Yard, they agreed not to pass the bill without hearing the weavers' counsel, and the bill itself was in the end unanimously rejected.[1]

In spite of the additional 20 per cent. *ad valorem* duty placed upon the East India goods in 1690, the condition of the weavers did not improve.[2] Partly, no doubt, the over-crowding of the trade, through the taking of too many apprentices, should be held responsible.[3] In 1696 'poor weavers' are especially mentioned in the instructions to the bishop of London to hold a house-to-house collection for the poor.[4] Their well-known poverty was considered likely to render them peculiarly open to Jacobite propaganda. In 1693 'numerous copies of a ballad exhorting the weavers to rise against the government were discovered in the house of the Quaker who had printed James' Declaration'.[5] But it was not until 1697 that the workers themselves introduced actual violence into the academic pamphleteering warfare over the question of the benefit and harm done by the East India trade. And their intervention proved more potent than the writings of such men as Pollexfen to inculcate protectionist ideas into the legislature. For, whereas the principal battle against the East India Company's activities had centred round its enemies' contention that its trade was

[1] *Parliamentary History*, v. 400–1; *Hatton Correspondence*, ii. 138–9; *L.J.* xix. 113–15.

[2] Stats. of Realm, 2 Will. & Mar., Sess. 2, cap. 4.

[3] Marshall, p. 196.

[4] *C.S.P. Dom., 1696*, p. 447.

[5] Macaulay, v. 444.

draining the country of its stock of precious metals, this plea was now reinforced by the cry that it was putting Englishmen out of work and so increasing the burden of the poor-rate.[1]

Again the trouble started through an attempt to exert pressure upon parliament, which was considering a bill for the limitation of the imports of East India silks.

The weavers and their wives, to the number, it was estimated, of four or five thousand, marched to parliament on 21 January 1697, filled the lobby of the house of commons, and were with difficulty kept out of the House by locking the doors. The city members were sent out to pacify them, and the sheriffs and justices sent for to order them to disperse, which they apparently did without causing any trouble. It has been suggested that there had been some agreement between the woollen-manufacturers and printers, owing to the presence of a prominent printer among the rioters. Probably they had other more highly placed allies, since it was noticed that the mob threatened no violence to any except opponents of the bill and that they seem to have had accurate information as to who the latter were. Luttrell wrote a few days later that the woman who rang the bell in Spitalfields to call the weavers together to go to parliament had owned she was hired for half a crown by another woman, a Roman Catholic, but there seems no other direct evidence of Jacobite influence upon the rioters.[2]

The House resolved 'that the inciting and encouraging any number of persons to come in a riotous manner either to hinder or promote the passing of any bill depending before this House, being against the constitution and freedom of parliament is a high crime and misdemeanour' and ordered a committee to inquire who had encouraged the mob. The Lords sent for the sheriffs, justices, constables, and watch to keep the peace; and, fearing further trouble, ordered the train-bands of Westminster to be out on the following day.[3]

---

[1] On the whole question of protectionism at this time see Heckscher, ii, pt. 3.

[2] *H.M.C. le Fleming*, p. 346; *Portledge Papers*, p. 249; Luttrell, iv. 174–5; Wadsworth and Mann, p. 132; A. Anderson, *Origins of Commerce*, ed. of 1787–9; ii. 633; *C.J.* xi. 667–8.

[3] *Parliamentary History*, v. 1163; Luttrell, iv. 172.

On the same evening, however, the mob attacked the East India house itself, broke open the outward door, smashed the windows, and pulled down the rails. The lord mayor and sheriffs, arriving with a guard, succeeded in dispersing them and in arresting three of their number. The secretary of state wrote on the same day to the lord-lieutenant of the Tower to have the militia of the Tower Hamlets in readiness, to the lieutenancy of London to see to that of the city, and to the duke of Bedford, as lord-lieutenant of Middlesex, to order the militia of Westminster to be prepared to suppress any further tumults. These precautions, and the repulse at the East India house, appear to have damped the rioters' spirits, and there was no more trouble.[1]

In March, when the Lords in their turn appeared hesitant over the bill, the weavers rose again and attacked a house in Spitalfields belonging to a member of parliament and deputy governor of the East India Company by the name of Bohmer. The train-bands came up (as also, according to Lapthorne, the king's guards) and fired upon them, killing two and wounding others, which caused the mob to disperse. The Commons at once voted an address asking the king to disperse the mob by the use of the militia or otherwise.

Two days later, upon the failure of the two Houses to agree, the bill was lost. The result was a further riot among the weavers, who got together in large numbers in the fields near Hackney and threatened the house of the famous merchant Sir Josiah Childs. The guards, however, were present to check them, and the press-masters took the opportunity of seizing several of the younger men who were going to join in the rioting, with the result that the mob once more dispersed.[2]

There would appear to have been rioting in the provinces as well, especially at Norwich, Canterbury, and Coventry.[3] But we lack for these any such graphic account as Defoe

---

[1] *Portledge Papers*, p. 249; Luttrell, iv. 174; *C.S.P. Dom., 1697*, p. 16. On 30 Jan. Luttrell recorded a new by-law of the weavers' company, that any of their journeymen taking part in such proceedings for the future should be disfranchised and given no more employment. Luttrell, iv. 177.

[2] Luttrell, iv. 199–200; *Portledge Papers*, p. 254.

[3] Anderson, ii. 646.

provides of the outbreak at Colchester in 1719 when the weavers of the East Indian fabrics were themselves assaulted by the mob.[1]

In April 1699, Luttrell recorded that the weavers in Spitalfields, being almost ruined by the importation of East India silks, had now resolved to make all sorts of stuffs, serges, &c., usually made at Norwich, Colchester, and Taunton, &c., which would be very prejudicial to those towns by reason of the Londoners' greater skill and close connexion with the merchants. In the same year, however, the prohibitory statute finally became law.[2]

Another trade which suffered from over-crowding was that of frame-work knitting, although in this case it was the effect of war upon trade, not competitive imports, which caused the trouble to become acute. In spite of the regulations of the charter of 1663, the Company refused to intervene to prevent the excessive taking of apprentices, doubtless partly owing to unwillingness to deprive the masters of the premiums paid. The result was a riot in which 100 frames were broken, some belonging to a master called Nicholson who had rendered himself particularly obnoxious, and in which some masters and apprentices were beaten. None of the rioters was punished, or even, it is said, apprehended, and the masters appear to have been sufficiently overawed by these proceedings to have agreed to abide by the rules.[3] Historians of the industry, however, date from this the removal of some of the masters and ultimately of the centre of the trade to Nottinghamshire, in order to avoid control. Wandering unemployed journeymen are said to have caused riots in other places besides London, the result being an act of 1727 making frame-breaking punishable with death, which led to an almost complete cessation of violence for forty years.[4]

---

[1] W. Lee, *Life of Defoe*, ii, 1869, pp. 136, 145; *V.C.H. Essex*, ii. 399.

[2] Luttrell, iv. 510; Stats. of Realm, 11 Will. III, cap. 3 and 10.

[3] Marshall, p. 197; W. Felkin, *A History of Machine-Wrought Hosiery*, 1867, pp. 73, 227; F. A. Wells, *The British Hosiery Trade*, 1935, p. 39; Chambers, p. 111.

[4] Felkin, p. 228; Chambers, pp. 89–100. For the frame-breaking riots in the midlands, where the Napoleonic wars caused another and more serious crisis in the industry at a time of increasing technological unemployment, see F. Darvall, *Popular Disturbances and Public Order in Regency England*, 1935.

In non-textile industries there is little to record during these years. In May 1711 the shoe-makers of London tumultuously petitioned parliament about the ruin of their trade through a rise in the price of leather owing to a draw-back being granted on its export.[1]

The nail-making industry, which was carried on in the villages around Birmingham and which provided a notori-ously bad example of the social conditions engendered by the 'domestic system', gave trouble in the summer of 1697 when a number of the nail-makers got into a body and marched in a tumultuous manner from place to place. The lords justices contented themselves with ordering the judges of the Oxford and midland circuit to inquire into the dis-orders, and to give directions for preserving the public peace.[2]

An example of the fear of technological unemployment outside the textile industries is the discontent which caused the first saw-mills in England to cease working in 1663.[3]

In August 1673 the apprentices and journeymen of the coach-makers and harness-makers of London supported a demand for a charter of incorporation by some not very formidable rioting. Here it is probable that their main object was to limit the number of new-comers into the industry.[4]

The dock-labourers of London and the other large ports were another group among whom trouble might have been expected. In London itself things were quiet, though in 1696 an effort of the city authorities to constitute a new fraternity among the labourers and porters employed in un-loading the Newcastle colliers was defeated by a lockout on the side of the merchants.[5] In Newcastle itself there was rioting among the keelmen—men employed in transporting the coal in small boats from the wharves to the colliers—and in 1710 they struck for higher wages. The civil magistrates were unable to deal with the strike, and troops were used to force the men back to work. A committee of the council

[1] H.M.C. Portland, v. 452, 454; Stats. of Realm, 9 Anne, cap. 12.
[2] C.S.P. Dom., 1697, pp. 240–1, 248.
[3] G. N. Clark, Science and Social Welfare in the Age of Newton, 1937, p. 97.
[4] P.C. 2. 64, p. 83; Letters to Sir Joseph Williamson, 1874, i. 172.
[5] Portledge Papers, p. 237.

was appointed to examine the causes of the dispute. Although their arbitration on this occasion brought about a settlement, further disturbances took place in 1719, 1738, and 1746.[1]

The tin-miners of Cornwall have already been referred to as a class particularly addicted to disorder. In spite of a loyal address which they presented to the new sovereigns in June 1689,[2] a prolonged depression in the tin trade soon provoked trouble. The depression had lowered their wages to such an extent that they had to undertake casual agricultural work in order to bring their incomes to subsistence level. In addition, the mines were often closed down altogether, during which periods begging and pillage were the workers' only resources.[3] In 1690, when the price of tin reached its lowest for the whole period, disturbances broke out among the miners.[4] The government issued orders for an inquiry to be made into the activities of those suspected of having carried on political agitation among them. In view, probably, of the possibility of an enemy landing being made in order to take advantage of the situation, two companies of troops were ordered to remain at Penryn. The lord-lieutenant, the earl of Bath, was informed that the council had discovered that the Cornish militia were in no condition to aid the civil magistrates, and was ordered to see that for the future care should be taken to have riotous meetings suppressed.[5] Thereafter peace seems to have been preserved, but when in 1703 the queen made an offer of royal pre-emption for the whole output of tin, a huge mob of miners surrounded the Convocation house at Truro and threatened the members with violence unless the offer were accepted. It is not possible to say whether this was in fact the reason for the acceptance of the royal offer.[6]

'The social conditions of the salt-workers', wrote an historian of the industry in the middle of the last century, 'have for centuries been, and in most cases continue to be a

[1] P.C. 2. 63, p. 37; *C.S.P. Dom., 1671*, p. 297; C.S.P. Dom., Anne, MS. p. 600; Lipson, ii. 127; E. R. Turner in the *American Historical Review*, xxvii; Nef, pp. 178–9.

[2] Luttrell, i. 550.

[3] G. R. Lewis, *The Stannaries*, 1908, p. 221.   [4] Ibid., p. 277.

[5] *C.S.P. Dom., 1690–1*, pp. 29, 34, 42.   [6] Lewis, p. 221.

reproach to English civilization.'[1] It is thus not surprising that a certain amount of disorder accompanied the revolutionary changes in the industry which occurred at the end of the seventeenth century. It was discovered in Cheshire, in 1670, that salt could be extracted from solid 'rock' and fully saturated brine, which could be mined, in place of the old method of evaporating surface brine.[2] The introduction of the new method into the various centres of the industry caused a great deal of litigation, and attempts were made by the old monopolists to secure government intervention to cripple the new method by either prohibiting rock-salt or by putting on a special duty, as was in fact done. The duty was not high enough, however, to prevent the expansion of the industry.[3] The consumer was protected by the justices' fixing the price of salt.[4]

In July 1694 one Robert Steynor, who had introduced the new method into Droitwich, found it necessary to protect his pits and wells by armed force, whereupon the town magistrates were given the usual instructions by the council for the suppression of the riots.[5]

In the record of the disturbances contained in this chapter there is little to provoke generalization. At the most, it can be said that these disturbances illustrate the strains set up in society by certain of the economic changes of the time. They do not appear to be disproportionate to the magnitude of the progress achieved, nor does the government appear in too unfavourable a light. It is, however, worth concluding with the remark that the worst off of all industrial

---

[1] *Industrial History of Birmingham and the Midland Hardware District*, 1866, ed. S. Timmins, p. 141.

[2] E. T. Ward, *The Salt Industry of Cheshire*.

[3] Stats. of Realm, 7 & 8 Will. III, cap. 31. On the whole dispute see E. Hughes, *Studies in Administration and Finance*, 1934, pp. 225–65.

[4] For examples of such action see *Buckingham County Records*, ii. 93, 106, 204, 247, 278, &c. In Cheshire, the main centre of the salt-mining industry, no actual disorder has been traced. There was, however, in May 1696 a mysterious riot in some copper-mines belonging to a certain Thomas Legh and his partner at Nether Alderley in that county. A band of men appears to have forced the workers out of the mines by using the windlasses which were part of the mining machinery to draw them up. As it was declared that Mr. Legh and his partner had enjoyed peaceable possession of the mines for three and a quarter years or more, it is impossible to state what the grievance was. Cheshire County Records, Sessions Roll, July 1696.　　　　[5] P.C. 2. 75, pp. 477–8.

workers appear to have been those in the naval dockyards. The clamours for payment of wages due, and the disorders in Portsmouth, Chatham, Woolwich, and Deptford in the years between 1663 and 1671 are an interesting illustration of the financial difficulties of which the defenders of Charles II have made so much.[1]

[1] *C.S.P. Dom.*, *1663–4*, p. 276; *1664–5*, pp. 463, 464, 480; *1667–8*, pp. 225, 226, 443, 455, 463, 473; *1671*, pp. 126–8, 348, 355, 364, 578.

V

THE FISCAL SYSTEM AND THE RECOINAGE

'THE acceptance in the seventeenth century', it has been said, 'of the doctrine that the poor should pay taxation is one of the landmarks in English political opinion.'[1] One might therefore expect that the shift in the incidence of taxation, begun when excise was introduced to pay for the Civil War and continued by the policy of the Restoration period, would have resulted in popular protest. 'He that gets his money by the sweat of his brow parts not from it without much remorse and discontent, and when all is done 'tis but a little they pay; therefore taxes that light heavy upon them (such as chimney-money and often-times a poll) tend rather to unhinge than assist the government.' So argues a writer of 1695.[2]

Of direct taxation of the poor there is little in the reign of Charles II. The poll-tax of 1660 was generally accepted, being a single payment and calculated to relieve the people of the hated burden of the army.[3] This, however, did little to recompense the government for the loss of revenue due to the abolition of the court of wards; and, as the secretary, Nicholas, was warned in November 1660, the result had to be an expedient which transferred the burden from the shoulders of the rich to those of rich and poor alike.[4] This was done by means of the hated hearth-tax or 'chimney-money', though the exemption of houses with only one hearth prevented the very poorest from being hit. The immediate unpopularity of this impost did much to increase the difficulties of the government in 1662, especially in the north of England, where money was scarce.[5]

Hostility continued throughout the lifetime of the tax,

---

[1] W. Kennedy, *English Taxation, 1640–1799*, 1913, p. 67.
[2] John Cary, *The State of England*, 1695, pp. 175–6.
[3] *C.S.P. Ven.*, *1659–1661*, p. 213.
[4] *C.S.P. Dom.*, *1660–61*, p. 361.
[5] Ibid., *1661–4*, pp. 120, 161, 180. On 14 Aug. 1662 the Venetian envoy, Sagredo, wrote from France that the tax had been repealed. This was untrue, but presumably the matter had at least been considered. Ibid., p. 259; Lister, *Life of Clarendon*, 1838, iii. 198.

manifesting itself in attacks on collectors which reached a climax in widespread rioting in 1666–7.[1] Even after this crisis there were complaints of oppression caused by the tax, notably again in the north.[2]

After the Revolution, William gained immediate popularity by removing the hearth-tax on the ground that it was 'not only a great oppression to the poorer sort but a badge of slavery upon the whole people exposing every man's house to be entered into and searched at pleasure by people unknown to him'.[3] Between the Revolution, however, and the settlement of the land-tax in 1697–8 there were still fairly frequent attempts directly to tax all classes.[4] There were poll-taxes in 1690, 1691, 1694, 1697, 1698, and additional taxation on servants' wages.[5] It was probably to direct taxation of this kind that Anthony Wood referred when he wrote in April 1692: 'The miners in Cornwall scruple to pay the tax.'[6]

They did not elsewhere provoke more than isolated instances of obstruction to their collection.[7]

It was not upon poll-taxes or chimney-money, however, that the governments of this period chiefly relied for their resources, but upon the customs and the excise. The introduction of the latter in the time of the Commonwealth had provoked almost immediate trouble. A riot at Smithfield in 1647, followed by other disturbances, produced the abolition of the excise on meat and the temporary cessation of that on salt.[8] Under the Commonwealth there were, indeed, several occasions when troops were used to quell riots caused by the unpopularity of the excise.[9]

The Restoration made the excise a permanent part of the fiscal system but did nothing to render it less odious, and it afforded a useful weapon to opposition speakers and writers.[10]

---

[1] L. M. Marshall, 'The Levying of the Hearth Tax, 1662–8', *E.H.R.* li, 1936.
[2] *C.S.P. Dom.*, 1675–6, p. 369.
[3] Stats. of Realm, 1 Will. & Mar., cap. 4.
[4] For the land-tax, E. Hughes, *Studies in Administration and Finance*, p. 168.
[5] Kennedy, p. 50.   [6] Wood, iii. 388.
[7] e.g. Cheshire County Records, Sessions Roll for Oct. 1689; P.C. 2. 73, p. 311; *Hertford County Records*, ii. 199; vii. 29.
[8] Kennedy, pp. 53–4.   [9] Hughes, p. 122.
[10] For a highly coloured description of its horrors see A. Marvell, *Poems*, ed. Margoliouth, p. 144.

There does not appear to have been any rioting against it in the reigns of Charles or James, but attacks on its collectors were not unknown.[1]

It was natural enough that the acute financial pressure of the French wars and the gap in governmental resources left by the abolition of the hearth-tax should have driven the statesmen of the Revolution to this expedient. Previous experience had taught them, however, the limits of its usefulness.

'Nothing would be more productive or less oppressive to the people', wrote the Brandenburg envoy, Bonnet, in November 1691, 'than a duty on the consumption of victuals and especially of meat, and yet nothing is so opposed by the majority of members [of Parliament] who fear either that if once established they would not have the power to repeal it when they desired to do so or that it would cause disturbances in places as has happened before.'[2]

But, although neither meat nor, with the exception of salt, other primary food-stuffs were touched, with direct taxation still not accepted as a regular source of revenue, and the customs disorganized by the war, reliance was of necessity placed upon the excise.[3] By 1714 the old duties on beer and its constituents had been largely increased, while new duties had been imposed on salt, candles, leather, soap, and coal, and on windows, paper, and spirits, as security for the interest of the new national debt.[4]

There can be no doubt that a great deal of discontent was aroused by this, and that passive resistance to the payment of excise may have been among the reasons for the large fall in the receipts from the hereditary (or single) excise upon beer, from £842,005 in 1689 to £533,580 in 1696.[5] It is possible, too, that the excise had some share in causing some of those riots which are known only from legal or administrative records and of the causes of which we have no knowledge. It appears, however, to have caused only one riot sufficiently important to attract the attention of the central governing body of the kingdom. The towns of Bishop's Castle and Montgomery were reported in January

[1] P.C. 2. 56, pp. 380, 411, 418, 441–2, 446–7.
[2] Quoted by Kennedy, pp. 58–9.   [3] Hughes, pp. 170–1.
[4] Kennedy, p. 57.   [5] Hughes, p. 184, n.

1699 to be the scene of 'illegal and riotous proceedings', when arrears of excise due from some of their inhabitants were demanded and levied. The council ordered the offenders to be prosecuted.[1]

Taxes upon salt have always been peculiarly objectionable; nevertheless, Mr. E. Hughes, in his study of the taxation of salt in England, notes 'the complete absence of any organized opposition' to the salt-tax after its re-imposition in 1694, although it was made perpetual in 1697, 'at many times the prime cost of the article'.[2]

The early acts had contained provision for price-fixing, which, as various entries in the Cheshire Sessions Book show, were actually put into force by the justices of that important producing county.[3] Nevertheless, evasion of the tax took place. In October 1695 Edward Fairchild, of Northwich, labourer, entered into a recognizance 'for selling salt loaves privately without paying the King's duty'. In January 1702 an order made against Daniel Barker for conveying salt without showing it to the proper officers was confirmed.[4]

The result was, in 1702, the creation of a special 'salt-office' for the collection of the tax and the prevention of evasions, it being stated in parliament at the time that in Droitwich alone 100 persons were actively engaged in smuggling with the connivance of the proprietors. The act of 1702 gave extensive rights of search to the officers appointed to secure the tax at its first removal from the works or the port of import. With the abandonment in the acts of the new reign of the price-fixing regulation,[5] smuggling became even more profitable and, no doubt, surer of the popular support on which that activity always depends. It certainly became more widespread and more violent in its methods.

There was a serious riot at New Quay in Cardiganshire in 1704 and at Conway in 1712, when a band of smugglers which attacked the salt-officer was led by a local justice of the peace.[6] In 1713 there was an assault made upon

---

[1] P.C. 2. 77, p. 295.　　　　　　　　　[2] Hughes, p. 178.
[3] Idem, p. 179; Cheshire County Records Quarter Sessions Book, Sessions of Apr. 1694, Apr. 1695, and Oct. 1695.　　　[4] Ibid., Oct. 1695, Jan. 1702.
[5] Hughes, pp. 179–92.　　　　　　　　　[6] Idem, p. 200.

searchers 'in the execution of their duty upon a seizure of some salt and horses coming from Scotland'.[1] It is not surprising that the salt-officer's life should come to be regarded as one in which risks were to be expected. In 1704 the salt-commissioners were actually asked to intervene to protect a man who had dangerously wounded one in the execution of his duty. The petition was undramatically endorsed ''twas not well done to fire bulletts'.[2]

Salt was, of course, not the only commodity whose smuggling led to violence. The collector and other officers of the customs of the port of Chester were attacked in 1700 at Mostyn in Flintshire by a 'company of men armed and in disguise, who removed out of the possession of the said officers a parcel of wine by them seized, beating, binding, wounding and miserably abusing the said officers until they had rescued and carried off or staved the said wines'.[3] There were attacks on customs officers during the reign of Charles II at places as far apart as Boston, Southampton, Colchester, and Penryn.[4]

The chief scene of violence in connexion with smuggling was always the south-east coast, and the commodity in question, wool.[5] On the whole, the prohibition of wool exports, intended at this period rather as a political measure against France than as part of an economic policy in the process of being abandoned, was popular with the country.[6] Indeed, the projected removal of the prohibition after the peace of Utrecht formed a main anti-government plank in the ensuing election. In Buckinghamshire, the whigs put wool in their hats, saying that it was all going to France and that they were resolved to have some of it before it was all gone.[7]

These sentiments naturally made less appeal to the population of maritime districts, and in Sussex and Kent the smuggling of wool was carried on throughout the period, to the despair of successive secretaries of state. Their anxiety was increased by the fact that a side-line of the

---

[1] C.S.P. Dom., Anne, MS., pp. 984–5.
[2] Ibid., p. 144. [3] P.C. 2. 78, p. 54.
[4] Ibid. 56, pp. 442, 449, 452, 455, 458–9, 471; C.S.P. Dom., 1679–80, p. 24; P.C. 2. 67, pp. 58, 65, 128, 153. [5] Bryant, pp. 161–2.
[6] See *supra*, p. 57. [7] *Wentworth Papers*, p. 351.

smugglers was the introduction into the kingdom of Jacobite agents and foreign spies, who could readily find shelter among the lawless population of Romney marsh until such time as their friends were ready to receive them.[1]

The political aspect of their activities may explain the peculiar violence which the 'owlers', as the smugglers of this district were called, so often displayed. In February 1696 the officers of the port of Rye were 'assaulted, beaten, wounded and put in danger of their lives' by a company of between thirty and forty fully armed men, some of whom were mounted.[2]

In October of the following year Capt. Baker, an officer charged with the task of supervising the prevention of smuggling in this area, gave an account to the lords justices of the acts of violence committed and was promised that some horse would be quartered there and would give him assistance. A few weeks later he presented to them a scheme for dealing with the whole problem, copies of which were ordered to be sent to the treasury, the admiralty, and the attorney-general. The attorney-general was ordered to undertake the defence of those employed in seizing the persons and effects of the 'owlers', pursuant to judgements given, against the vexatious actions which had been brought against them.[3] In September 1698, following a petition received in July, the lords justices issued a proclamation for the enforcing of the laws against the export of wool, wool-fells, &c. It stated that the laws had been evaded and that wool, wool-fells, &c., had been exported both to Scotland and overseas not clandestinely but openly by bodies of armed men who had attacked the customs officers.[4] In the following months many arrests are recorded.[5]

The problem did not, however, cease to disturb the authorities, and in 1702 a variety of schemes appear to have been submitted for dealing with it, both to the admiralty, which disclaimed responsibility, and to the commissioners

---

[1] *C.S.P. Dom.*, *1663–4*, p. 531; *1670*, p. 8; ibid. *Will. & Mar.* and ibid. *Anne, passim.* For the efforts of the secretaries of state to control the ports of entry from France and the Low Countries, see Chap. VII, *infra.*

[2] P.C. 2. 76, p. 287. [3] *C.S.P. Dom.*, *1697*, pp. 439, 466.

[4] Ibid., *1698*, p. 394; P.C. 2. 77, pp. 197 and 235–9.

[5] *C.S.P. Dom.*, *1698, passim.*

of customs.[1] There was certainly justice in the provision in the proclamation of 1698 that the penalties statutorily recoverable from the inhabitants of the maritime or border counties through which the smuggled goods passed should be made effective,[2] for the whole thing was really a question of policing limited areas where conditions were made harder by the sympathy of the local population with the smugglers.

For rioting due to real and widespread popular discontent we have to look elsewhere. The financial aspect of the great recoinage of William III's reign is a part of the general financial history of the country. There is almost certainly truth in the contention that the crisis was one of credit, and that the state of the coinage was only the most obvious of its symptoms.[3] The rapid approach of such a crisis had been foreseen earlier in the reign. Among various memoranda of the period dealing with the financial stringencies of the administration, there is one of August 1692, by Lord Rochester. He is so sceptical as to the possibility of raising further large sums in taxation as to suggest that a new and less costly foreign policy is essential. An anonymous marginal commentator adds that the Lord Privy Seal, the earl of Pembroke, says that he thinks the allies could make a defensive war only, and that if William were to 'make a great descent into France, Parliament would give any thing or if that could not be done, then you should let them know you would take care the money should circulate as much as may be here, for buying clothes, bread, and all that is possible to be bought here at home.' The commentator adds that the carrying of money abroad for the army's wages is a great grievance.[4]

Side by side with more grandiose projects for monetary reform there was a good deal of activity directed towards stamping out the ubiquitous crime of coining. But the

---

[1] *C.S.P. Dom., Anne*, i. 233–4 and 516–20.

[2] P.C. 2, loc. cit. Luttrell wrote on 22 Sept. 1696 that it was reported that the principal inhabitants of New Romney and other Kentish towns were leaving on account of this provision. Idem, iv. 113.

[3] J. E. T. Rogers, *The First Nine Years of the Bank of England*, 1887, chap. i; W. R. Scott, *English Joint-Stock Companies*, 1912, i. 348–9; iii. 208–9.

[4] *C.S.P. Dom., 1691–2*, pp. 410–12.

frequent arrests and executions proved useless.[1] So bad was the state of the coinage that the succession of high-price years in William's reign was partly attributed to this cause.[2] The condition of the smaller coins was such that people were reluctant to take them, and in January 1694 the Northamptonshire sessions made an order to the effect that those refusing half-pence and farthings should be bound over.[3]

The recoinage was essential if a permanent improvement was to be sought. But the deflationary process which it involved, coming as it did at a time of exceptional scarcity, hit the mass of the people very hard indeed. The method of calling in the bad money which was finally adopted meant that those who were most fitted to bear the burden were those who chiefly escaped it,

'the landowners with land and property tax to pay, the tax-collectors, the bankers, the stock-jobbers, and the well-to-do middle class people of the towns who could subscribe to loans and annuities. These had not only been able to unload upon the Exchequer any stock of bad money they possessed, but in many cases, no doubt, had made a nice profit by purchasing clipped money at a discount from less fortunate persons.'[4]

Nor was this fact wholly hidden from contemporaries. As late as November 1696, when the worst was over, a Rochester correspondent of Sir Joseph Williamson's wrote of the discontent of those in the country at the apparent resolution of parliament to rob them of their old broad money when there was such a lack of the medium of exchange. He remarked that it was a very obvious truth that the vast sums of money that had been coined in the last two reigns had been drained away from them in a few years, and asked why nothing should please them except a species of money it was plain they could not keep and which the goldsmiths could keep and the merchants export with so much advan-

---

[1] For an account of the methods employed by coiners see *H.M.C. Kenyon*, pp. 185–6. For measures taken to deal with coiners, see *Portledge Papers* and Luttrell, *passim*.

[2] For example, admittedly largely for polemical reasons, by C. Davenant in *An Essay on the East India Trade*, 1696.

[3] Northamptonshire County Records, Sessions Minute Books, Jan. 1694.

[4] A. E. Feaveryear, *The Pound Sterling*, 1931, pp. 128–9.

tage to themselves. (He suspected incidentally that the exigencies of the exchequer would cause the new money to be called in in the following year.)[1]

The position was aggravated by the action of the receivers of the land-tax, who were reported to the lords justices in July 1696 to have paid in the whole assessment in clipped money although it had not yet been collected from the parishes. It was asked whether they could now recover it by distress from those who were in arrears. They were, since the money was to come to them, more pressing than they would otherwise have been and had besides injured the state by paying in clipped money what they would receive in new coin. An inquiry was ordered, and it was thought fit that some of them at least should be made examples of. But the lords of the treasury proved unwilling to postpone payment of the receivers. They were also unready to change them as they thought this would only increase the already sour humour of the people against paying the residue of the taxes.[2]

It is thus against a background of profit-making and peculation, as well as of ignorance and tory or Jacobite propaganda, as emphasized by Macaulay, that we must envisage the outbreaks of popular discontent between May 1696 and March 1697, by which date the recoinage operation was virtually complete.[3] Apart from the immediate scarcity there was, too, a permanent loss of money to be faced. 'The recoinage', writes Feavearyear, 'is said to have cost the State £2,700,000. There seems to be no doubt that at least another million of loss fell upon the holders of clipped coin, mostly the poorer people.'[4] In the then stage of the country's economic development this was a huge sum.

Even before the fateful 2 May, the last day on which the clipped money was current, when crowds besieged the

---

[1] C.S.P. Dom., 1696, p. 443.

[2] Ibid., pp. 255 and 376; H.M.C. le Fleming, p. 343. It would appear that it was the southern counties which were affected.

[3] Macaulay, vi. 177–204. Feavearyear's criticism of Macaulay's account of the recoinage (p. 131, n. 2) appears on the whole to be justified. He does not mention the fact, as Feavearyear notes, that for a large portion of the clipped money the state paid only 5s. 8d. per ounce or less, and he thus neglects the inequality of treatment which the poorer classes received.   [4] Feavearyear, p. 130.

exchequer to pay their taxes, signs of distress became apparent.[1] Mr. Cartwright, Lord Lexington's agent, wrote to the latter from his Nottinghamshire estates:

'I have not yet taken Mr. Clay's [the Steward's] accounts, for as yet he does not venture to receive any money; for guineas which were current at thirty shillings are now twenty-five shillings, and all silver so bad that we all live on trust, except for ale, where any money passes, the excise-men having orders to receive such.'[2]

In Shropshire the Jacobites were reported to be gaining credit among the mob by taking brass and clipped money as payment, presumably of rents.[3]

In May the position became more serious. Prices rose, and Lapthorne, wrongly prophesying a plentiful year for all things, remarked that graziers would not bring their cattle to town by reason of the scarcity of good money. The goldsmiths were again the villains of the piece, refusing to bring forth their best money and trying to put the people off with clipped coin.[4] By the beginning of June the probable failure of the land-bank project had added to the financial confusion.[5] The attention of the authorities was also distracted from the growing distress in the country by the succession of Jacobite conspiracies then coming to light.[6]

At a meeting of the lords justices on 16 June it was reported from Plymouth that there were difficulties about paying the soldiers their subsistence in money. It was directed that the soldiers should exact their subsistence in money but take it in provisions. They further resolved upon a proclamation to the effect that the people might remedy their difficulties by submitting to disposing of bad money by weight.[7] Elsewhere unemployment added to the pre-

---

[1] Macaulay, vi. 166. On 8 May the governor of the Bank of England had to speak to appease the crowds demanding the new money at the Bank. Luttrell, iv. 55.

[2] *Lexington Papers*, pp. 174–5, letter of 24 Feb.

[3] Martha Harley to Sir Edward Harley, 13 Feb. 1696; *H.M.C. Portland*, iii. 574.   [4] *Portledge Papers*, p. 230.

[5] Rogers, p. 62. As late as 6 June Lapthorne expected the land bank to succeed, basing himself on the information in the *Gazette*, and he hoped that money would then be plentiful. On 15 June he wrote, 'The land bank is likely to come to little.' The project was abandoned on 31 July. *Portledge Papers*, pp. 232 and 236.

[6] Chap. II, *supra*.   [7] *C.S.P. Dom., 1696*, p. 227.

vailing trouble. On 27 June the lords justices took into consideration a direction of the king's for holding the Norfolk assizes at Thetford instead of Norwich. They decided that if the assizes were not held in Norwich none of the gentlemen would attend, and it would in all probability occasion a great disturbance in that city. Trouble was hardly restrained already by reason of the clipped money and the unemployment among the 'manufacturers'.[1]

The worst effects of the scarcity were, however, felt in the poorest part of the country, the north.[2] Here, too, the state of the coin had been worse than elsewhere, as is amusingly illustrated by the difficulties of a Westmorland undergraduate in Oxford, who found the money he had brought from home of very little use.[3]

On 6 June Sir John Lowther anxiously inquired of Sir Daniel le Fleming as to the state of trade at Kendal and the fairs, saying that he feared the new money would come very slowly into the county unless it was supplied by the drovers and the southern customers.

Three days later there was an outbreak at Kendal, caused by the excise collector refusing most of the money offered him as not being conformable to law. A great many of the mob were ale-house keepers and, according to one of le Fleming's correspondents, half drunk. They went to the mayor and demanded how they were to get bread if their money would not pass. The mayor and le Fleming's informant tried to pacify the mob by saying that they would accept all money not clipped within the innermost ring, in their dealings, and hoped others would do the same. The mob remained unsatisfied and moved about the town making a great noise. Le Fleming's correspondent added that as the discontented were far too strong for the civil power they gave them some drink, and got them to promise not to molest the town that night but to have a 'frolic in the country'. They could instead, he declared, do nothing but give them good words lest there should be bloodshed.

[1] *C.S.P. Dom., 1696*, pp. 247–8.

[2] For the poverty of the northern counties compared with the rest of England see Ernle, p. 146; Marshall, pp. 94–5.

[3] See vol. iii of the correspondence published by the Oxford Historical Society under the title of *The Flemings in Oxford*.

On the next day Viscount Lonsdale reported that the militia were to be held ready to march to Kendal if necessary. The rioters, however, spent the day roaming the surrounding country in search of subsistence and plunder. The authorities thus had time to pull themselves together, and they arranged for a watch of 48 men to be set that night, to consist of an alderman and 15 selected men in each street. By eight o'clock the rioters were already back and assaulting the town guard. The recorder, who attempted to appease them, was knocked down but succeeded in rising and in rallying his supporters. After an hour's fighting the mob began to give way, the guards securing twenty of them. Writing the next day, a certain W. Brownsword informed le Fleming that they would keep fifty men under arms until the militia came. He described their position as very distracted and frightful, with the mob threatening to beset Lowther and Rydal. On the twelfth the militia came in and marched the prisoners to Rydal.

It is not surprising that, on 15 June, le Fleming wrote to Lowther that he had never known the country in a worse condition. This was occasioned chiefly by the coin. He remarked on the stringency felt by the poor and on the height of prices.[1]

At Halifax there was further trouble. An exciseman was knocked on the head and his money taken from him. Of the Sheffield area, the duke of Norfolk wrote to the lords justices that the gentlemen there were against the refusal of clipped money that was punchable.[2] In Newcastle there was also a riot, though here a political suspect was reported to have been discovered among the mob.[3] Shrewsbury, the secretary of state, congratulated the mayor and magistrates upon suppressing this tumult, remarking that he had no doubt but that the return of their fleet of colliers would bring them an immediate supply of current money and expressing the wish that the necessities of other parts of the country could be so soon provided for.[4] Writing on 16 June to Blathwayt, the secretary-at-war, Shrewsbury showed

---

[1] *H.M.C. le Fleming*, pp. 343–4; *C.S.P. Dom.*, *1696*, p. 227.
[2] Ibid.; *H.M.C. Buccleuch*, ii. 252.
[3] Luttrell, iv. 70. [4] *C.S.P. Dom.*, *1696*, p. 221.

himself still despondent. He did not see that it was possible to find an effectual remedy which would not have the effect of encouraging the bad coin to pass again.

'When another quarter of the land-tax and more specially the window-money comes to be paid,' he wrote, 'I fear the people will very unwillingly part with their heavy money and keep that which is clipped and will not pass since they have got the notion in their heads that the King has a recompense for changing all the little money, and that the window-tax is intended for that purpose.'

After mentioning the disturbances at Kendal and Halifax he concluded:

'We must expect the same accounts from other places and unless the Mints which are designed to be set up in four or five different places, will serve to amuse the people, I know not what else can, and they will not be ready yet this month.'[1]

It was to be considerably more than a month before the new provincial mints began seriously to improve the situation. Meanwhile the government felt called upon to take action. On 2 July the lords justices issued a proclamation, which was circulated to the counties, ordering the justices of the peace to consult how they might relieve the labourers and the poor 'in the present great difficulty in the exchange of money'. They were also to inform themselves of unusual meetings, such as had lately taken place, and to disperse such of them as they thought dangerous to the public peace.[2] The Middlesex justices decided to hold petty sessions monthly for both the above purposes.[3]

The country was still by no means quiet. The justices had been informed of the danger of a serious insurrection among the miners of Derbyshire should their clipped money be refused.[4] There was also a warning from the justices of Staffordshire that disturbances might occur there.[5] A letter from the Somerset justices also arrived enclosing a petition from the town of Taunton. It was ordered that

[1] *H.M.C. Buccleuch*, ii. 252.

[2] *C.S.P. Dom.*, *1696*, p. 257; Crawford, p. 501; Luttrell, iv. 80; *Wiltshire Quarter Sessions Records*, pp. 280–3.

[3] *Middlesex County Records.* p. 156.

[4] Feavearyear, p. 129. The Derbyshire miners had a good insurrectionary record. See E. Bernstein, *Cromwell and Communism*, 1930, p. 168, for their activities in 1649.

[5] *C.S.P. Dom.*, *1696*, p. 283.

they should be acquainted with the directions given by the treasury about the receivers' being easy to the country, and about the new mints.[1] These warnings of the probability of further serious disorder produced a concession. In July an order was issued permitting people to pay their clipped money into the exchequer as a loan at 5s. 8d. per ounce, instead of into the mint, where they only got 5s. 2d. The money began to come in at once.[2] On 1 August, however, Lapthorne remarked that the people still generally complained for lack of money, although the mint in the Tower was constantly at work, and it was said that work had started at the new provincial mints.[3] Shrewsbury endeavoured to allay apprehension by pointing to the latter fact. Nevertheless the danger of disorder was not yet passed, as can be seen from a warning which Secretary Trumbull received from the Liverpool authorities on 19 August.[4]

By now the 5s. 8d. was being paid for clipped money brought to the mint, and in September an order was issued by which this price was to continue to be given until 4 November.[5]

In October, when political passion was being roused by the rumour of important disclosures by Sir John Fenwick, parliament discussed the disorders.[6] John How, the member for Cirencester, gave the house on 28 October 'such an account of his county as if it were all in tumult, and greater were to be feared, for which he was told since there was so little of it in other parts of the kingdom, they wished there were no fomenters of it there'.[7] No doubt other members were correct in saying that the discontent was being capitalized for political reasons. A few days later a proclamation was issued offering a reward of £500 for the discovery of the author of a 'false and scandalous libel entitled an account of the proceedings of the House of Commons in relation to the recoining the clipped money and falling the price of guineas'.[8]

Much of the discontent was real enough. An act was

[1] *C.S.P. Dom., 1696*, p. 286.
[2] Feavearyear, p. 130.
[3] *Portledge Papers*, p. 236.
[4] *C.S.P. Dom., 1696*, pp. 342 and 352.
[5] Feavearyear, loc. cit.
[6] See Chap. II, *supra*.
[7] Vernon to Shrewsbury, 29 Oct. 1696, *Vernon Correspondence*, i. 30.
[8] Crawford, p. 503.

passed in November by which hammered money was to be received at the mint until 1 July 1697 at 5s. 4d. an ounce, and in payment of taxes and loans until 1 June at 5s. 8d. Broad hammered pieces were to be received by tale until 18 November. But this measure did not find universal popularity.[1]

Yet it is true that by now the worst period of scarcity was over and with it the greatest economic crisis of the period. Once again we have seen the inadequacy of the civilian authorities to deal with popular tumults, and noted the empirical concessions to necessity made by a government largely unaware of the nature or magnitude of its economic problems.

[1] Feavearyear, p. 130; *C.S.P. Dom., 1696*, p. 443; *Portledge Papers*, p. 242.

VI

THE ARMY, THE NAVY, AND THE PEOPLE

(a) THE ARMY

IN the final chapter, it is hoped to show that the armed
forces were used to a greater extent, perhaps, than is
generally realized in the suppression of the popular disturbances of the period under survey. Nevertheless, in spite
of the high moral tone taken up by its political opponents,
they were not merely concerned for the political liberties
of the people.[1] Naturally the sight of Dutch troops guarding
the king of England was galling to the national pride.[2] But
the rooted hostility shown them had the same foundation
as that shown against the native English regiments. The
antagonism to a standing army, which became a political
tradition in England, can only fully be understood if considered against a background of continual if petty conflicts
between the military and the civilian population.[3]

The low character of the army's personnel caused its
members to be viewed with suspicion wherever they were
stationed. 'The overflowing scum of our nation is listed',
runs a letter of 1678. Every time peace was concluded and
a portion of the army disbanded it set free a crowd of
marauders with no hope of earning an honest livelihood.
Many of them, in January 1679, for instance, 'sayd they
would robb for home they durst not go'.[4]

The horrible conditions prevailing on active service made
recruiting difficult. In cases of unwillingness to serve, or
of desertion, popular sympathy was invariably against the
military, and this sometimes showed itself in actual violence.
The attitude of the civilian authorities, especially of the
country justices, was often such as to encourage these outbreaks.[5] Of the navy, much the same might be said, though

---

[1] For the arguments brought forward against a standing army, see the account
of a commons debate of Nov. 1685, *Reresby Memoirs*, p. 396.   [2] Ibid., p. 545.
[3] Macaulay, vi. 289–91, 310–13.   [4] *Verney Memoirs*, ii. 325–6.
[5] The attacks made upon the army by parliamentary orators in 1697 provoked
not unnaturally fierce resentment among its ranks, and only the action of the king
in ordering officers to their quarters seems to have prevented this resentment from
taking an active form. Macaulay, vi. 311

here the tradition of impressment went back farther and aroused less suspicion, and such trouble as did occur was for obvious reasons confined almost exclusively to seaport towns.

Leaving aside, therefore, for the present the question of the use of troops in suppressing riots arising from economic or political causes, the present chapter will deal with those disturbances with which members of either of the services were directly concerned.

The grievances about billeting had, of course, played a prominent part in the political controversies of the reigns of the first two Stuart kings, but had only arisen at times when some foreign expedition made the assembly in one place of large numbers of soldiers and sailors a necessity. The history of the standing army can only be dated from the period of the Commonwealth. Under Charles II, too, the army was, as we have seen, particularly prominent in the suppression not only of political opposition, but of religious dissent, and had, while employed for these purposes, claimed, with the support of the Crown, to be exempt from the authority of the civilian magistrates, and to owe obedience to the Crown alone, acting through the military authorities. 'The Army', says one of its historians, 'thus became an instrument of coercion to the people who were unable to appeal to the legal tribunals of the kingdom for protection or redress against their oppressors.' At the same time the practice of billeting became, in the face of the government's poverty, a continuous, instead of an intermittent, necessity and in this way a permanent grievance.[1]

The Disbanding Act of 1679 declared billeting illegal.[2] These provisions were, however, violated throughout the reign of Charles's successor, and billeting was even enforced in private houses when public-houses lacked room.[3] The reason was not so much the wish of the government for a permanent 'dragonnade', as an insufficiency of barracks. Every temporary augmentation of the army meant, unless

---

[1] C. M. Clode, *The Military Forces of the Crown*, 1869, i. 54–5. For complaints of this see *C.S.P. Dom.*, *1663–4*, p. 553; *1672–3*, pp. 32 and 243; *1672*, pp. 449, 478, 534, 550.

[2] Stats. of Realm, 31 Car. II, cap. 1.   [3] Clode, i. 80–1.

billeting were resorted to, that the troops were put under canvas, causing large losses from desertion, and in times of adverse weather even larger ones from disease.[1]

It is thus possible to argue that 'the billeting of a large standing army was probably the greatest social evil endured by the people when William III reached England'.[2] In January 1689 a proclamation prohibited the quartering of troops in private houses without the consent of the owner —a consent which it is difficult to imagine as often forthcoming. Quartering in public-houses was to be carried out under the direction of magistrates and constables, not under the direction of the army officers themselves.[3] An act of the same year of the same import as the proclamation excused itself by referring to the necessities imposed by the Irish rebellion.[4] As we know, however, peace was far off, and so 'what was admitted with extreme caution as a temporary expedient, became, no doubt, a permanent arrangement'.[5] It is, however, said that the power of billeting was not compulsory until the act 10 Anne, cap. 13. In the act 12 Anne, cap. 13, an express limitation was imposed as follows:

'That the Act should not compel the quartering of any officer or soldiers, unless it be within ten miles of the palace or place of Her Majesty's usual residence, or within ten miles of the place where Her Majesty shall be present, or in some garrison or garrisons when sufficient barracks are not provided for them or unless it be in the marches of such officers or soldiers, and that in such marches no person shall be obliged to quarter them more than six days at a time.'

This clause had been necessitated by the refusal of the Westminster authorities to billet the guards in Westminster

[1] Ibid., pp. 221–3; *Hatton Correspondence*, i. 166–7, for desertion from Blackheath camp in 1678.

[2] Clode, i. 229. For the friction caused by the billeting of troops in York under Charles II and James II, see *Reresby Memoirs, passim.* For rioting in 1678 between undergraduates and dragoons quartered at Oxford, see *C.S.P. Dom., 1678*, pp. 183–4; *The Flemings in Oxford*, i. 236.

[3] Crawford, p. 475.

[4] Stats. of Realm, 1 Will. & Mar., Sess. 2, cap. 4. Cf. 2 Will. & Mar., Sess. 2, cap. 6, cl. 18. The justices were also empowered to fix the prices which soldiers were to pay for provisions. Even the power of the civil authorities was carefully limited. After an opinion on that subject had been given by the justices of Hertfordshire several constables were fined in 1695 for billeting soldiers outside their own parishes. *Hertford County Records*, i. 424.

[5] Clode, i. 231.

as not being troops upon the march according to the provision of the act 6 Anne, cap. 74.[1]

A good deal of friction took place before the necessity of billeting was accepted.[2] The measures already referred to, for disarming the opponents of the new régime and restoring order in parts of the country where the period of the Revolution had been marked by particular turbulence, caused clashes between the military and civilian authorities, though the actions of the military were often felt to be excusable on grounds of necessity.[3] The earl of Drogheda, commanding the troops engaged in searching for arms in Cheshire, denied that they had committed depredations among the game but confessed that they had taken a few trifles through ignorance of their rights. He complained that a guard which he had sent to look after the house and park of a certain unpopular Roman catholic named Massey were looked upon as an oppression and that he intended to withdraw them. He was very bitter about the extortionate prices charged by the inhabitants of Chester to his men, and complained that, although they paid cash for everything, the soldiers were universally disliked and that only the intervention of Lord Delamere had enabled him to get quarters for them at all.[4]

The right of the local justices to fix the prices which soldiers were to pay for provisions was not denied.[5] But there seems to have been some reason for the complaint

---

[1] Clode, i. 231–2. For an order concerning the quartering of the foot guards in April 1703, see *Middlesex County Records*, p. 257. There was a movement under James II to cut down the numbers of garrisons. Some appear in effect to have been abandoned. *Reresby Memoirs, passim.*

[2] Proclamations ordering troops to pay for quarters and commanding officers to inform magistrates that no credit was to be given, prohibiting threats or violence or the disturbance of game by soldiers, ordering officers to give redress for complaints, and prohibiting billeting in private houses without the owners' consent, were issued in 1691, 1694, 1695. This shows that the government was at least not unaware of what was going on. Crawford, pp. 488, 491, 497.

[3] *C.S.P. Dom., 1689–90*, p. 131. There had been a conflict at Bristol in Feb., between the mayor and the officer commanding the troops quartered there, over the custody of the town keys. Shrewsbury intervened in favour of the former. Ibid., p. 10.

[4] Ibid., pp. 165–6.

[5] See, for such schedules, *North Riding Quarter Sessions Records*, vii. 106, 149; *Buckingham County Records*, i. 380–1; ii. 324–5.

about Chester, since, in March 1690, the justices were ordered by Shrewsbury to have the charges for quartering reduced on the grounds that 6*d.* a night was beyond the means of a foot soldier.[1] Complaints, however, came from the other side as well, and in 1692 Clarke, the secretary for war, was forced to accede to a petition of the Westminster innkeepers that they should receive 8*d.* a night as they had done under Charles II, though he refused to let them claim for arrears on that scale.[2]

The fear of not being paid at all also played its part in stimulating apprehension, in spite of previous efforts by the military authorities to allay it.[3] In Totnes and Dartmouth, in 1693, there were complaints that sick seamen had un-justifiably been quartered on the inhabitants, and that the men could not be properly cared for while their quarters were so poorly paid. The report to the secretary of state throws a severe light on the prevailing conditions when the writer remarks that those who complain should remember that in those parts they had been paid off till that summer's expedition, whereas at Portsmouth the authorities had only paid for quarters up to June 1692 and at Rochester and Chatham stood indebted for about two years.[4] Not only provisions but damage caused had to be paid for. In October 1692, on the occasion of the army's passing to Ireland, the Liverpool accounts contained a payment of £4 10*s.* 0*d.* to 'Alderman Richard Windall for several goods the soldiers burnt and spoiled in his house near the Exchange'.[5] But while municipal authorities may have intervened to secure payments due to prominent citizens, humble people must in individual cases have suffered severely. There is among the Cheshire records a pathetic petition from the wife of one Peter Norbury of Neither Tabley. The latter had bought a public-house upon mortgage, and, having 'but little stock to begin with, and so many of King William's and Queen Mary's Armes quartering free and not paying', had been unable to meet his debts, and had joined the army

---

[1] *C.S.P. Dom.*, *1689–90*, p. 493.

[2] Ibid., *1691–2*, pp. 431, 442. For a petition for payment from one of them, ibid., p. 467.

[3] Clode, i. 44.   [4] *C.S.P. Dom.*, *1693*, p. 33.   [5] Picton, i. 341.

in Ireland in order to avoid imprisonment, since when nothing further had been heard of him.[1]

It is not surprising, therefore, to find in the years after the Revolution a succession of complaints from various parts of the country about the conduct of troops quartered upon the inhabitants and, as in the case of Penryn in 1696 and of Berwick in 1697, asserting that the locality had been totally impoverished.[2]

The town which suffered most was probably Portsmouth, which was at once a military centre and a naval base. In May 1689 a petition from the municipal authorities and the citizens complained that the town, being a garrison, had 'suffered much by soldiers left behind their colours, by their wives and children when they die or march, by debts they contract beyond their pay, but particularly by the great disorders lately committed by the Irish, who not only made themselves masters of the houses by free quartering but threatened to destroy the petitioners which it is believed they would have done'.[3] The removal of the Irish did not end the trouble. In April 1692 the mayor refused a request from a lieutenant-governor to quarter sixty men in public-houses on the ground that it was illegal, for though 'they could not say there was any law against it, yet there was no law for it'. This argument appears to have puzzled Nottingham, then secretary of state, who asked for the attorney-general's opinion on it.[4] In 1695 there appears to have been serious disorder between the military and the citizens.[5] Matters were not helped by the distrust for each other of the civil and naval authorities, which was symbolized in May 1697 by the former's having to break down the dockyard gates, which had been closed against them during their annual perambulation of the bounds.[6] This unwillingness of the civilian authorities to co-operate with the armed

---

[1] Cheshire County Records, Sessions Roll for Jan. 1690.

[2] For Penryn, see *C.S.P. Dom.*, *1696*, p. 200; for Berwick, ibid., *1697*, pp. 190–1. See also ibid., *1689–90*, pp. 156, 164; *1691–2*, pp. 316, 319, 325; *1696*, p. 200; *1697*, pp. 359–60, 405.

[3] Ibid., *1689–90*, p. 108. There had been trouble between the mob and the military authorities on the occasion of a great fire there in 1682. Ibid., *1682*, pp. 451, 464–5, 473.   [4] Ibid., *1691–2*, p. 239.

[5] Ibid., *1695*, pp. 55, 64.   [6] P.C. 2. 77, pp. 21, 29.

forces was almost universal. One can only chronicle as an exception Secretary Trumbull's letter in October 1696 to the mayor of Reading, thanking him for assisting in quartering troops there.[1] Such antagonism, of which many examples might be given, and which we shall notice again in connexion with recruiting and impressment, is the more remarkable when we remember the readiness of the civil authorities to have recourse to military aid in cases of popular disturbances.[2]

A series of incidents, trivial in themselves, illustrates the continuing antagonism of the people to the army. In January 1692 there was some disorder at Cambridge between the scholars and the officers of Lord Cutts's regiment over the drinking of a royal health.[3]

In July 1692 it was thought best to reprieve a soldier condemned for murder at Kingston assizes, for this reason, among others: that there might be disorder if the execution took place while the regiment was still quartered at Kingston.[4] In March 1693 there was a disturbance at Oakham, in Rutlandshire, between a company of foot soldiers and some butchers.[5] In June 1695 some soldiers, including an officer, assaulted a Coventry alderman.[6] In June 1702 the inhabitants of Dartford not only refused to quarter a regiment, but attacked it and wounded some of the soldiers.[7] In August 1710 a farmer in the Isle of Wight had his house plundered by soldiers after shooting one of them who was robbing his orchard.[8]

The internal history of the army is outside our sphere, but it is worth recording, besides the important mutiny at Norwich in March 1689, various other disorders among the troops in this period.[9] There were mutinies at Blackheath in 1673, at Canterbury in 1674 and 1679, and at Ashford in 1674. Under William III there were mutinies at Berwick in August 1691, at Bideford, during an embarkation, in February 1698, and among soldiers quartered near Staines

[1] C.S.P. Dom., 1696, p. 417.   [2] See Chap. VII, infra.
[3] Luttrell, ii. 330.   [4] C.S.P. Dom., 1691–2, p. 372.
[5] Luttrell, iii. 63.   [6] C.S.P. Dom., 1694–5, p. 506.
[7] Ibid., Anne, i. 111.   [8] Luttrell, vi. 618.
[9] For the effect of the Norwich mutiny and its connexion with the subsequent passing of the Militia Act, see Clode, i. 142.

in March 1709.[1] Defoe severely censured the conduct of the party opposed to the government in openly rejoicing at the mutiny among the marines which took place at Canterbury in December 1713.[2]

The part of the civilian population in the tumults of the soldiery was not always a passive one. In May 1695 there was a disturbance among the troops at Northampton which was apparently fomented by the townspeople.[3] The punishment of soldiers by martial law was always resented by the people. In December 1695 five troopers of the earl of Macclesfield's regiment quartered at Coventry, who had been imprisoned for disobeying orders, were released by the townspeople.[4] In July 1696 there was a riot at Gloucester on the occasion of the execution of the sentence passed by a court martial upon some soldiers there.[5]

Similarly the deserting soldier could always rely on popular sympathy. Desertion, facilitated by the lack of proper barracks, was always a serious problem for the military authorities.[6] Enlisted men were rescued in London in June 1674.[7] In July 1695 there was a riot at Loughborough with the object of freeing two arrested deserters.[8] In November of the same year a mob of two or three hundred attacked some soldiers who were being conducted from New Sarum to Stockbridge, to such effect that twenty-seven of the soldiers were able to desert in the confusion.[9] In Cheshire, in 1696, the attempted arrest of a soldier who had 'overrun his colours' was met with threats of open resistance by his relatives, and no doubt such incidents could be multiplied from other local records.[10] Furthermore, juries would not convict deserters when caught.[11]

---

[1] *Hatton Correspondence*, i. 110; *Letters to Williamson*, i. 83; P.C. 2. 64, pp. 191, 194; *H.M.C. Portland*, iii. 473; *C.S.P. Dom., 1698*, p. 115; C.S.P. Dom., Anne, MS. p. 500.

[2] *H.M.C. Portland*, v. 376.   [3] *C.S.P. Dom., 1694-5*, p. 470.

[4] Ibid. vii. 1.   [5] P.C. 2. 76, p. 475.

[6] See, for instance, Nottingham's letter of August 1692 ordering care to be taken to prevent the soldiers in the Isle of Wight deserting and escaping thence by boat. *C.S.P. Dom., Will. & Mar.*, p. 425.

[7] P.C. 2. 64, p. 242.   [8] Ibid. vi. 3.

[9] *Wiltshire Quarter Sessions Records*, p. 282.

[10] Cheshire County Records, Quarter Sessions Roll, July 1696.

[11] For such an incident at the York assizes in 1687, see *Reresby Memoirs*, p. 445.

Such incidents were, however, merely the by-products of the two essential facts of the situation, the unpopularity of the wars among the masses of the people and the prevailing system of recruiting. The latter was altered by the act of 1703–4 and its successors, which for the first time made legal the conscription for land-service of the able-bodied unemployed.[1] It is therefore convenient to treat the periods before and after the change separately.

Nevertheless, the system of recruiting prevailing down to that date can only with difficulty be dignified by the name of voluntary. It is true that it was admitted that there was no legal basis for impressing men for the land-service. Enlistment was, however, freely offered as an alternative to imprisonment for debt or fines for small offences.[2] In February 1691 there were complaints from Kent that some army officers had been impressing several farmers and their servants. Viscount Sidney, then secretary of state, wrote to the mayor of Canterbury asking for particulars of the persons concerned in order that redress might be given and such practices prevented for the future. He asserted categorically that such practices were entirely disapproved of by their majesties, that they were expressly against the law, and that legal redress could be obtained for them.[3] In the same month, however, he wrote to the lieutenant of the Tower demanding the release of a lawyer's clerk who had been impressed, not on the ground that impressment was illegal, but merely on that of the particular individual's unsuitability.[4] In December of that year a stranger called upon to give an account of himself to the magistrates of Deal declared him-

---

1 Stats. of Realm, 2 & 3 Anne, cap. 13; 3 & 4 Anne, cap. 10; 4 & 5 Anne, cap. 21; 6 Anne, caps. 17 and 45; 7 Anne, cap. 2; 8 Anne, cap. 13; 9 Anne, cap. 4; 10 Anne, cap. 12; Trevelyan, *England under Queen Anne,* i. 218–19.

2 There are several such incidents among the Northamptonshire Quarter Sessions Minutes. Cf. *Buckingham County Records,* ii. 453. During the recruiting campaign of 1672 nothing could be got at Aylesbury but 'gaolbirds, thieves, and rogues'. *Verney Memoirs,* loc. cit. For a plan, ultimately rejected, to recruit men for Tangier by enlisting them nominally for service at Plymouth and then decoying them on shipboard, see *C.S.P. Dom.,* 1665–6, pp. 69–70, 77.

3 Ibid., *1690–1,* pp. 246–7. A Northamptonshire recognizance of 1694 orders two men, one of them a victualler, to appear to answer charges made against them 'particularly for compelling them [their accusers] to goe for souldiers without their free consent, contrary to the rights and freedom of Englishmen'.

4 Ibid., p. 269.

self to be the officer of a regiment in Flanders come to recruit men. 'I told him', writes the secretary of state's informant, 'there was no such warrant granted to press landsmen; then he knew not what to say.'[1] The above incidents all point to the conclusion that the actual state of the law was vague and not universally understood, and that recruiting officers, finding it hard to make up their full complement by persuasion or bribery, were not above using force.

There is indeed no lack of actual evidence that such was the case. In March 1691 Viscount Sidney, one of the secretaries of state, was actively engaged in checking statements to the effect that at Bristol threats were being used to obtain men to serve in Ireland.[2] In case of invasion all citizens were of course liable to serve. In April 1692 Wood records a press in Oxford for 'idle fellows to fight against the French about to invade England', and states that about twelve such were obtained in Oxfordshire—no very formidable force.[3]

The methods of the provost-marshals whose job it was to fill up the gaps in their regiments were thus regarded with justifiable suspicion. A house in Holborn, used nominally for the detention of deserted sailors, was actually kept by an Irishman named Tooley who was provost-marshal to Lord Cutts's regiment. It was used as a place of detention for offending soldiers and also as a place where men who had been cajoled or bullied into joining the army, or had had the king's shilling pressed upon them when drunk, were kept until they could be shipped to Flanders.[4] As it was reported that Tooley sold them to commanders at £3 per head, it is not surprising that he was suspected, probably with justice, of making use of kidnapping methods in order to add to his profitable trade.

On 9 April 1695 the sheriff of Middlesex had an execution to make against Tooley. His entrance into the house

[1] C.S.P. Dom., 1691–2, p. 47.
[2] Ibid., 1690–1, pp. 307, 314, 326.
[3] Wood, iii. 388; Luttrell, ii. 425. In the Chester Sessions Roll for July 1696 there are certificates that certain persons have found substitutes for their own service in the army, but it is not clear upon what their obligation to serve had been based.
[4] C. Walton, History of the British Standing Army, 1660–1700, 1894, pp. 483–5.

was resisted by some of the soldiers, and he was forced to seek assistance. He was thereupon joined by a mob which was swollen by numbers of people who had been indulging in recreation in Lincoln's Inn Fields. They entered the house and that of another provost-marshal in Holborn, and in spite of armed resistance, which resulted in a number of them, variously estimated at from one to six, being killed, succeeded in rescuing the prisoners and destroying the goods and furniture. The mob proved unruly for several nights more, and both the train-bands and the guards were called out to deal with them. They further attacked a small prison in Finsbury, but the recruits, normally kept there, had been removed. This seems to have been the full extent of the damage, but as usual the popular fears outran reality. 'It was said', wrote the under-secretary, James Vernon, to Lord Lexington, 'they threatened to set open all the prisons; and if they did so those that are in them would show them the way to open all other houses.'[1] Nevertheless, apart from Vernon, the contemporary accounts of the riots—Lapthorne's, for instance—are chiefly remarkable for the utter lack of surprise or indignation which they manifest. The England of the period was most certainly a callous country.

As might be expected, the recruiting acts of Anne's reign met with fierce opposition inside and outside parliament, though in fact they did little more than render universal existing practices. Opposition grew in strength as enthusiasm for the war waned, and it culminated in January 1709 in the rejection of the government's proposals for extending the system.[2]

The acts, it was true, were limited in their application to 'such able-bodied men as have not any lawful calling or employment or visible means for their maintenance'. But

[1] *Lexington Papers*, pp. 75–6; *Portledge Papers*, pp. 199–200; *Hatton Correspondence*, ii. 216; *H.M.C. le Fleming*, p. 335. In July Tooley was tried for murder but acquitted (Luttrell, iii. 494), and in July 1698 a petition from him praying an allowance of £1,319 10s. 0d. for his losses at the hands of the mob was referred by the council to the treasury. P.C. 2. 77, p. 203. It is interesting to note Vernon's anticipation here of what was to be the chief horror of the Gordon riots, the indiscriminate emptying of the London prisons.

[2] Trevelyan, *The Reign of Queen Anne*, ii. 387; iii. 34. This was the first defeat in the house of commons sustained by any ministry of Queen Anne's. W. S. Churchill, *Marlborough*, iii (1936), pp. 350–1.

in fact the decisive word rested with the local justices—
though civilian jealousy is shown in the provision that
justices with military posts could not act under it. The
power thus conferred on the justices meant that employers
could use the threat of conscription against their recalcitrant
employees without the latter having any possibility of appeal.[1]
The rights of constables and other parish officers to search
for people liable to serve under the act must also have lent
themselves to abuse, and the provision in the act of 1708
for the payment of £3 to the overseers of the poor in each
parish for every recruit raised within it must have strained
their consciences to breaking-point.[2]

The fact that the definition as to who were liable for
service was being extended is shown by the fact that the act
of 1704 definitely exempted harvest-workers, whose work,
if irregular, was both lawful and necessary.[3] In one act of
1705 it was found necessary to ensure, under stringent
penalties, that no one should be drafted to serve except
by a definite number of justices.[4] Victimization, where
one or two justices only had acted, must have been
frequent.

The administrative records, central and local, show that
these acts were actively put into effect, but the difficulties
attending their execution are apparent.[5] Instructions to put
the act into effect were sent in the form of letters from the
privy council to the holders of the usually combined offices of
custos rotulorum and lord-lieutenant of the several counties.[6]
In March 1708 the county of Middlesex and the cities of
London and Westminster were especially assigned as recruiting grounds for the two regiments of foot guards, and the
officers of those regiments were ordered to meet the justices

---

[1] For this and an account of some abuses in the act's administration see
Trevelyan, i. 219.

[2] See the acts cited *supra*, p. 115, n. 1. Nominally the money was to help, if
necessary, the dependents of the enlisted men.

[3] Stats. of Realm, 3 & 4 Anne, cap. 10, cl. 10.

[4] Ibid., 4 & 5 Anne, cap. 21, cl. 8.

[5] The MS. calendar of the State Papers for the reign of Queen Anne lists many
documents dealing with recruiting and its difficulties.

[6] For Buckinghamshire see Hamilton, op. cit., p. 275. Such a letter dated
5 Dec. 1706, and addressed to the duke of Marlborough as Custos Rotulorum of
Oxfordshire, is among the Oxfordshire Lieutenancy Papers.

in order to take over their recruits.[1] In July 1709 a proclamation suspended the payments made under the acts to
parish officers and churchwardens for recruits, as sufficient
men had been obtained.[2] But this happy state of affairs did
not last long, and in December 1710 St. John, the secretary
of state, was asked by George Granville, then secretary for
war, for a renewal of the circular letter about recruiting.[3]

Evidence of the class of men recruited under the acts can
be obtained from local records. Those of Derbyshire are
particularly revealing. 'Vagrants' were naturally the first
category. In November 1703 debtors were released from
prison on promising to enlist or find substitutes. In 1704 a
felon was forgiven two crimes by the quarter-sessions court
on condition of his enlistment.[4] Such recruits were not the
prerogative of any one county. The Hertford gaol calendar
contains an entry, dated 1 October 1705, to the effect that
one Richard Wells was committed for want of sureties for
good behaviour, 'he being a dangerous person', to remain
until next sessions or 'untill he shall be taken into her
majesty's service as a soldier by the Captaine under whom
the Court is informed he is listed'.[5]

For this type of recruit the army provided a not wholly
undesirable opening, but even the poorest members of the
non-criminal part of the population did their best to avoid
service. In 1705 a 'chirurgeon' of Buckinghamshire successfully petitioned the court for payment for his services in
curing a vagrant who had deliberately disabled himself in
order to avoid service.[6]

In order to secure recruits strange devices had to be
adopted. In 1709 there was a complaint that several seamen
in Middlesex had been impressed for the army instead of

[1] *Middlesex County Records*, p. 324.
[2] Crawford, p. 500.
[3] C.S.P. Dom., Anne, MS. p. 633.
[4] Cox, pp. 223–8. The requirements were lowered as the difficulties of recruiting
became greater. The privy council's usual circular letter contained in Jan. 1708
the following addendum: 'Her Majesty has likewise thought it fit to Direct that the
officers do not too exactly insist on the usual standard provided the men are well
sett and of strength sufficient for the service.' Oxfordshire Lieutenancy Papers.
[5] *Hertford County Records*, vii. 61. For the enlistment of a tinker, followed by a
dispute between two parishes as to his wife's settlement, see ibid., p. 50.
[6] Hamilton, p. 276.

for the navy.[1] Furthermore, the central government had to contend with the often hostile attitude of the local justices, who, in many cases, disliked the war and also objected to military officers' themselves conscripting men direct. A statement of their attitude can be found in the charge to the Essex grand jury at the sessions of July 1705.

'If anyone', declared the chairman, 'take up a land-man and don't carry him before a Justice and pursue the late Act of Parliament (tho' with a Warrant) I take it to be a Misdemeanour and breach of the Peace and presentable by you; if it were lawful before this Act were vain. The Parliament were so tender on this point as to make it probationary, and that too for a very short time; it is making away that which is much dearer to a man than his Goods, and next to his Life, his Liberty, and perhaps carrying him where the Queen's writ can't be executed, and if he have an Action when he can, even if he comes home, it is such a remedy a poor Man had as good be without.'[2]

Obstruction was not confined to speeches. Trouble arose in January 1703 (before the first of the recruiting acts of the reign was passed), when the justices of Cumberland arrested an army captain for enlisting a man contrary to law. The latter declared the man to have been properly enlisted. 'Nor', he said, 'do I think the Justice of Peace has anything to do with this case. If they do I perceive the Queen would get few soldiers.' Only a court martial could, in his opinion, release the recruit.[3] At Ipswich in March 1703 some justices came among the commissioners for enforcing the act, abused them, and released some recruits.[4] At Reading in February 1711 the constable was arrested for putting the recruiting laws into action.[5] Sometimes it was difficult to see whose was the fault. In 1706 Lieut. Massey, who was supposed to be superintending impressment in Middlesex, complained of the justices' remissness. They asserted that on the contrary it was he who had neglected his duties.[6]

With such confusion prevailing among their superiors

[1] *Middlesex County Records*, p. 352.

[2] N. Corsellis, *A Charge to the Grand Jury at the Quarter Sessions for Essex at Chelmesford*, July 1705 (a pamphlet in the Corpus Christi College, Oxford, library). The recruiting acts were each for one year and were re-enacted annually from 1703 till 1711.   [3] *C.S.P. Dom., Anne*, i. 542, 274.   [4] P.C. 2. 82, p. 277.

[5] C.S.P. Dom., Anne, MS. p. 660.   [6] *Middlesex Sessions Records*, p. 301.

it is not surprising that popular resistance to recruiting was more marked than ever. A whole series of riots marks the years in which the acts were in force. In June 1704 there was a riot near Coleshill in Warwickshire occasioned by an officer's seizing a young man on the pretence that he was a deserter. The local constable was among the rioters, one of whom was badly wounded. 'This part of the country', wrote a correspondent to Harley, the secretary of state, 'has yearly supplied the army with very great numbers of men whose friends are dissatisfied with the death of some and abuses that many others of them have met with abroad in former times.' Unless, therefore, the officers were made an example of, recruiting in the future, he declared, would be very difficult.[1]

Recruiting was not hard in Warwickshire alone. From Exminster Long Street in Devon came a report in November 1704 of an attack upon an ensign who had arrested a deserter.[2] In February 1705 the deputy mayor of Pembroke refused to intervene against a riotous gathering which was attempting to rescue an 'idle fellow with no visible means of living', impressed for the army.[3] In August an attack was made by a mob of over twenty persons upon some soldiers who were conveying to Southampton a 'disorderly fellow' enlisted by the justices of Romsey.[4] In 1706 there was serious rioting, at Newbury in January, and at Abergavenny in September. So strong was the popular feeling in the latter town that it was impossible to collect information against the rioters. The lukewarmness of the authorities was primarily blamed for the triumph of the populace, which, it was said, would, unless checked, make recruiting there permanently impossible.[5] In May 1707 a recruit was rescued at Leigh in Gloucestershire.[6]

Deserters still offered a problem. In 1708 a special clause was inserted in the recruiting act of that year to include among those to be impressed a band of deserters who were gathered in a place called Threapwood, near Cuddington, on

---

[1] *H.M.C. Portland*, viii. 123–4.   [2] C.S.P. Dom., Anne, MS. p. 159.
[3] *H.M.C. Portland*, viii. 169.   [4] C.S.P. Dom., Anne, MS. p. 244.
[5] For the Newbury riot, *H.M.C. Portland*, viii. 279, 281. For the Abergavenny riot, ibid., p. 335.   [6] C.S.P. Dom., Anne, MS. p. 442.

the borders of Cheshire and Flintshire. The commissioners appointed for Cheshire under the act and the officers of Cuddington seem to have shirked this task, and the clause was re-enacted three years later.[1] Perhaps no incident of the period better illustrates the weakness of the administrative machine.

(b) THE NAVY

'A man would be thought ridiculous', wrote Admiral Sir George Rooke to Shrewsbury from Cadiz in February 1696, 'to undertake to charge a well-formed battalion with a crowd of rabble, and I protest, my Lord, such a mob is the generality of this fleet manned withal.'[2] Yet the task of obtaining men for the fleet, even of this low quality, was one of the heaviest which faced the governments of the period.

'In England', writes a modern historian, 'the French practice of recruiting galley-slaves by the aid of the law had its counterpart in the practice of pressing people into the navy, which lasted down to the beginning of the nineteenth century.'[3] As we have seen, it was for the manning of the land forces rather than the sea forces that the criminal law was employed at this period. The enforcement of the obligation to serve in the navy was merely a partial enforcement of the general obligation of defending the country. In spite of the reforms of Pepys and of James II when duke of York, who have both received such liberal praise from recent writers, the navy did not by any means yet afford a desirable career, and compulsion was necessary. Naturally, the chief source of supply was found in the ranks of the merchant seamen, although this damaged the country as a whole by the obstacles which it placed in the way of trade, which was already suffering from the ravages of privateers. In the summer of 1702, when the outbreak of the war of the Spanish succession caused the maximum amount of activity

---

[1] Stats. of Realm, 7 Anne, cap. 2, cl. 25; 10 Anne, cap. 12, cl. 26.

[2] *H.M.C. Buccleuch*, ii. 301. We have an account of the men impressed in Worcestershire in the summer of 1702. They were 'thirty-two very sorry fellows' who would only 'lie in the scuppers at sea and be "nautious" [*sic*] to the ship's company' they joined. Three had been discharged at once, two being lepers, and the other aged and infirm. *C.S.P. Dom., Anne*, i. 199–200. Cf. *C.S.P. Dom., 1664–5*, pp. 236 and 240; *1671–2*, pp. 315–17.

[3] Heckscher, ii. 300.

in the direction of securing men for the navy, the experiment was even tried, with little success, of placing an embargo upon the coastal trade in order to secure men for the fleet. A letter from Whitehaven on 27 May made it clear that its chief effect was to warn men away from the coast towns. People expected there that, when the convoy of ships for which they were waiting arrived, they might get more men, 'for the high wages offered in war-time always bring out men whom neither the press-gang master nor the civil magistrate can find'.[1] This declared reliance on financial inducements to join the navy cannot, to judge from the government's actions, have been very seriously meant.

Merchant seamen were not the only people liable to impressment. Fishermen, it is true, having for the most part families dependent upon them, were not impressed except at a time of acute emergency.[2] Bargemen, however, a class growing in numbers, with the increasing attention being paid to improving inland water-transport, were specially liable to be seized.[3] In September 1696 'thirteen west-country bargemen were tried for killing two press-masters who had boarded a barge off Lambeth, and acquitted, it appearing their warrant was not legal'.[4] Sometimes the needs of the navy conflicted here with the even more pressing needs of the civilian population. In 1691 protection from impressment was granted to six men who were absolutely necessary for the working of the ferry-boats between Fulham and Putney.[5] The admiralty wished to go even farther and

---

[1] On the suffering caused by the non-payment of seamen's wages see Ogg, i. 252–4. The wages had been fixed during the Commonwealth and remained at the same level, in spite of changes in the price-level, till 1797. Dobree and Mainwaring, *The Floating Republic*, ed. of 1937, p. 32. There were petitions about the arrears of pay due to seamen and complaints that this hindered naval enlistment throughout the period. See, e.g., *C.S.P. Dom., 1665–6*, p. 314; *1667–8*, p. 304; *C.S.* xiii. 230–1. For 1702 see *C.S.P. Dom., Anne*, i. 89.

[2] J. R. Hutchinson, *The Press-Gang, Afloat and Ashore*, 1913, p. 98. In 1690–1 the impressment of seamen in colliers was prohibited. P.C. 2. 74, pp. 135 and 156.

[3] Willan, pp. 110–11.   [4] Luttrell, iv. 81, 101.

[5] *C.S.P. Dom., 1689–90*, p. 423. The calendars contain other cases of intervention by the secretary of state to prevent people being impressed, which show similar abuses to those noted in connexion with the recruiting acts. In 1707 there were complaints that the justices of Cambridge were impressing men and discharging them upon payment. C.S.P. Dom., Anne, MS. p. 485.

to secure an act of parliament making liable to impressment not only seamen and watermen (including those of the Thames), but also surgeons, gunners, house-carpenters, coopers, hoymen, or carmen, with exception only for those who had served as volunteers for a certain number of years.[1] In June 1702 it was suggested to the treasury that there were a great number of men employed in the customs-house sloops who might be drafted into the navy, since the number of privateers was making their immediate occupation of little use.[2] Certainly the local authorities responsible do not seem to have been over-scrupulous as to whom they impressed. In 1673 there were complaints of damage done to farming by the impressment of men from the fields.[3] In the year 1706 there was very acute anxiety with regard to the state of the fleet and particular attention was paid to impressment.[4] In February the Huntingdonshire justices reported that they had issued their warrants to search for 'straggling seamen, watermen, lightermen, bargemen and fishermen', and that very few were to be found. They added that they might find several able-bodied men belonging to none of these categories who would be serviceable on board and desired to be directed how to dispose of them.[5]

An effort was made to overcome these difficulties by setting up a system of registration. In spite of the fact that one of the inducements to enrol was eligibility for the services of the newly founded Greenwich Hospital, the register, which was nominally in force from 1696 to 1710, was a failure.[6] One of the things urged in its favour in a debate in parliament in 1698 was that it would save the great expense and trouble of pressing men, which caused general complaint.[7]

To the seamen, however, this expedient seemed to make impressment more certain than ever and it was a fate to which they had never been reconciled. At the beginning of the second Dutch war, perhaps the only war of the period for which there was some measure of popular support, men

[1] C.S.P. Dom., 1693, 440.
[2] Ibid., Anne, i. 98.
[3] Ibid., 1673, p. 376.
[4] Luttrell, vi. 25–9.
[5] H.M.C. Manchester, p. 46.
[6] Hutchinson, p. 22.
[7] C.S.P. Dom., 1698, p. 429.

were obtained for the fleet without much difficulty.[1] But by 1666 there are accounts of men fleeing from the ports in large numbers to avoid impressment.[2] In 1672 the difficulties of securing men were felt at once. To avoid being pressed in Bristol, men fled to Somersetshire and Gloucestershire, where the power of the Bristol justices did not extend. As in the previous war, many took refuge in the Kentish weald. Some travelled still farther afield. Heads of houses in Oxford were directed to see that men fleeing from the press did not hide in undergraduates' rooms.[3]

The same difficulties occurred in William's reign. In April 1692 the lords justices of Ireland were ordered to see ✓ that sailors on ships bound thither returned, lest they should attempt to avoid impressment by making for the plantations.[4] In February 1696 the lord-lieutenant of Kent was ordered to stop seamen accepting minor parish offices in order to avoid impressment, and to put guards on all the roads leading from the Kentish ports to London.[5]

The tendency of seamen to 'straggle', that is to say to seek refuge inland, made the co-operation of the civil authorities of the inland counties necessary if the men were to be secured.[6] This was by no means always forthcoming, and there were complaints of apathy and even of active opposition to the government's measures.[7] Other means having failed, Nottingham advised the commissioners of the admiralty to send trustworthy officers to help with the work.[8] The lesser county officials were no doubt the chief offenders. A letter from the council to Viscount Weymouth, the custos rotulorum of Wiltshire, dated 31 December 1696, which gives comprehensive orders for impressing men for the

[1] Ibid., *1664–5*, pp. 40, 44, 243–4.

[2] Ibid., *1665–6*, pp. 453 ff. In the previous year orders had been given that pressed men should not be allowed to hire substitutes. Ibid., *1664–5*, p. 265.

[3] Ibid., *1671–2*, pp. 136, 183, 302–3.

[4] Ibid., *1698*, p. 429.

[5] P.C. 2. 76, p. 288; *C.S.P. Dom.*, *1696*, p. 53.

[6] All press-warrants had to be endorsed by a justice of the peace, though originally this provision only extended to fishermen. Hutchinson, p. 97. The co-ordinating authorities for impressment were the 'vice-admirals' of the maritime counties (usually the same individuals as the lord-lieutenants).

[7] *C.S.P. Dom.*, *1665–6*, p. 469; *1673*, pp. 443–7; and the correspondence of the vice-admiral for Yorkshire, *H.M.C. Var.*, *Coll.* viii. 72–7.

[8] *C.S.P. Dom.*, *1691–2*, p. 236.

navy, contains the following warning: 'And your lordship is to take care that the respective officers, within the said county do their duty in the service, many of whom 'tis apprehended do not only forbear the execution of these orders but do conceal the seamen that fly from the press.'[1] The statute of 1705, ordering justices and municipal authorities to make regular searches for concealed seamen, is unlikely, in view of this, to have had much effect,[2] and the offer, in a proclamation of 1708, of a reward of 20s. for every straggling seaman taken up appears as a counsel of despair.[3]

In view of the attitude of the civil authorities, the institution of some form of professional impressment authority was probably essential, although the form it took was scarcely one likely to raise the tone of the navy.[4] The conduct of the press-gangs was never such as to make for the peace of the town where their activities were carried on, and the authorities of at least one such port, Deal, complained to the vice-admiral, Carmarthen, that they had always produced their quota without such aid and asked to be relieved from the depradations of the gangs.[5] Not least of the troubles was the rivalry between rival gangs, each seeking men for their own ship, such as led to open fighting in Portsmouth in May 1705.[6]

Men secured under such circumstances were not easy to handle. In 1666 special legislation was passed to prevent and punish the disorders arising among them on pay-days.[7] Many minor disturbances among the seamen are recorded. More notable was the rescue of some sailors, arrested for seditious words, from Newgate in December 1666, since this riot reached such formidable proportions that the guards were called upon to quell it.[8] In William's reign Jacobite agitators sought to make use of the sailors' grievances. 'Un-

---

[1] *Wiltshire County Records*, p. 283.
[2] Stats. of Realm, 3 & 4 Anne, cap. 10. [3] Luttrell, vi. 386.
[4] For the activities of the press-gang, see Hutchinson, op. cit., chap. viii. The negative attitude of the authorities was not confined to inland towns. In March 1706 the mayor of Kingston upon Hull and a sergeant of that town took the lead in opposing the naval press-master. *H.M.C. Portland*, viii. 219–21.
[5] Hutchinson, p. 197. [6] Ibid., pp. 189–91.
[7] Stats. of Realm, 18 & 19 Car. II, cap. 12.
[8] *H.M.C. Portland*, iii. 303.

happily,' writes Macaulay, with good reason, 'the vices of the naval administration furnished the enemies of the State with but too good a choice of inflammatory topics. Some seamen deserted: some mutinied: there came executions; and there came more ballads and broadsides representing these executions as barbarous murders.'[1]

No propaganda was needed to give rise to the disturbances caused by the system of impressment. In the years 1666 and 1667 there is case after case of the riotous rescue of pressed men and of violent opposition by all classes to the activities of the gangs.[2] 'My people', wrote Pepys on 28 March 1668, 'tell me that the want of men will be so great as we must press; and if we press there will be mutinies in the town; for the seamen are said already to have threatened the pulling down of the Treasury Office; and if they once come to that it will not be long before they come to ours.'[3]

Pepys's forebodings were unjustified, but the resistance to impressment continued. Cases of the riotous rescue of impressed seamen come from Norfolk in 1691 and from Hertfordshire in 1693.[4] In 1693 a gunner of the fort at Margate not only refused to assist the commander of a ship to impress seamen, but raised a tumult among the people in order to prevent his doing so.[5] Attempts to press apprentices led to riots in London in 1691 and 1706.[6] Most striking of all was the report in May 1702 that in Sussex the seamen fearing impressment were flying to the woods, and gathering 'into bodies able to resist the country'.[7]

There was, we have seen, little active co-ordinated resistance to the war measures of the government in this period, but it is obvious that the cumulative effect of the disturbances must have been quite considerable. It is worth noting, too, that they are not evenly distributed throughout the fifty years. The first of Charles's wars against the Dutch was

---

[1] Macaulay, v. 444.
[2] P.C. 2. 59, pp. 233, 481, 497, 510, 513; *C.S.P. Dom., 1666–7*, pp. 333–4, 509.
[3] *Pepys's Diary*, 28 Mar. 1668.
[4] P.C. 2. 74, p. 149; *Hertford County Records*, i. 404.
[5] P.C. 2. 75, p. 147.
[6] *C.S.P. Dom., 1691–2*, pp. 139, 213; Hutchinson, p. 175.
[7] *C.S.P. Dom., Anne*, i. 84.

obviously fairly widely welcomed. According to a letter of 24 October 1664, there would have been volunteers enough against the Dutch if only they were to have been fought against in home waters and not in Guinea.[1] No succeeding war enjoyed this measure of approval. But the naval drain was the only one large enough to cause serious worry in the reign of Charles himself.

With the French wars of William we get a steadily increasing demand for men for the land service leading up to the acts of Anne's reign. And in the opposition which they aroused we may see at least one of the causes which paved the way for the tory victory on a peace cry and so ultimately for the peace policy of Walpole.

[1] *C.S.P. Dom.*, *1664–5*, p. 40.

VII

POPULAR DISTURBANCES AND THE MACHINERY OF THE STATE

'The Reason and End, and for which all Government was at first appointed was
to prevent Disorder and Confusion among the People; that is, in few words to
prevent Mobs and Rabbles in the world.'

DANIEL DEFOE, Preface to *Hymn to the Mob*.

'THOUGH every man who has entered into civil society, and is become a member of any commonwealth, has thereby quitted his power to punish offences against the law of nature, in prosecution of his own private judgement, yet with the judgement of offences, which he has given up to the legislative in all cases, where he can appeal to the magistrate, he has given a right to the commonwealth to employ his force for the execution of the judgements, of the commonwealth, whenever he shall be called to it, which indeed are his own judgements, they being made by himself or his representative.'[1] This positive conception of the duties of a citizen, presented by the typical political theorist of the period, had its counterpart in law. Each citizen was personally responsible for assisting in the preservation of the peace, and was liable for penalties if he neglected this duty. The special statutory powers and responsibilities of justice, sheriff, and constables rested in the last resort upon this fundamental principle of the common law.[2]

For the prevention of minor breaches of the peace the officer immediately responsible was the constable, whose powers originated in the common-law powers of the township, 'but when the law was more closely examined it was found that his actual powers for the preservation of the peace differed very slightly from those of the lieges who were not indued with the dignity of office'.[3] His presence did not, indeed, release the individual citizen from his responsibilities. 'In the execution of his duty the constable could

---

[1] J. Locke, *Two Treatises of Government*, ed. of 1764, pp. 270–1.

[2] Sir William Holdsworth, *History of English Law*, viii. 330–1. The best general introduction to county administration in this period is S. A. Peyton's introduction to the *Kesteven Quarter Sessions Proceedings*.

[3] H. B. Simpson, 'The Office of Constable', *E.H.R.* x, 1895. Cf. Peyton, pp. l–liii.

demand help in his Majesty's name, or by showing his magistrate's warrant, from any person, and could present such a one for trial at Quarter Sessions if he refused to give it.'[1]

It is not easy to say how far the village constable at this period was an efficient officer. No office filled by a combination of election and rotation, and wholly unpaid, can have been popular with its holders. Some of the duties attached to it, those, for instance, in connexion with the laws of settlement, were arduous and unpleasant; some, such as searching houses for poaching instruments, might be dangerous.[2] It is not surprising that the presentments of constables for the non-performance of their duties bulk very large in local records.[3] There is at least one case of a refusal to be sworn constable on the ground that it was not the turn of the individual in question.[4] A fairly low standard is suggested by the entry in the North Riding records for July 1690, that the treasurer for Richmondshire was to pay to the constable of Tunstall 15*s.* as a gratuity to encourage his future diligence, he having formerly apprehended several dangerous persons when he was upon the watch.[5]

Foreign observers do not appear to have been impressed by the constables. F. Bonnet, the Brandenburg envoy, writing of the Commons' opposition to their being given greater powers in connexion with recruiting, describes them as 'des gens aisez à corrompre'.[6] During this period, too, it became necessary for the justices, especially in the more urbanized districts, to exercise their permissive power of appointing a constable in cases where the court leet no longer acted.[7] Another symptom of the decline of the con-

[1] E. Trotter, *Seventeenth Century Life in the Country Parish*, 1919, p. 92. There are indictments in the Buckinghamshire records for refusals to help constables.

[2] Only the very poor could successfully claim exemption from the office. For one such case see *Hertford County Records*, vii. 5. Cf. Peyton, loc. cit.

[3] *North Riding Quarter Sessions Records*, *passim*; Deposition of Prisoners in York Castle, *Hertford County Records*, vii. 49; Cheshire County Records.

[4] Cheshire County Records, session of May 1689.

[5] *North Riding Quarter Sessions Records*, p. 111. The same records contain notices referring to gratuities paid to private citizens for apprehending suspects. Ibid., pp. 153 and 195. Cf. *Buckingham County Records*, ii. 87.

[6] Ranke, vi. 242.

[7] Stats. of Realm, 13 & 14 Car. II, cap. 12; Simpson, p. 63; Dowdell, p. 18.

stable into a purely subordinate officer, a delegate of the
justices rather than a trustee of the powers of the township,
was the growing practice on the part of the petty constables
of making their presentments to quarter sessions through the
chief constable of the hundred instead of directly through
'constable juries'.[1]

The chief constables, the officers of the hundred, were
still responsible for the keeping of the peace within that
area and for the setting in motion, where necessary, of the
old machinery of the Hue and Cry, though their precise
relation to the petty constable is obscure. The chief constables, too, like ordinary citizens, were urged to help keep
the peace by the additional consideration that the liability
for damage done would fall on the hundred. For the settling
of such suits and the collecting of the rate involved fell upon
them, though there seems no trace among printed records
of a rate levied on a hundred in this period to recompense
the sufferers from a riot.[2] There are several payments,
however, to persons robbed. There is also an account by
Lapthorne of an attempt by a Somersetshire grazier to
obtain money from a hundred by pretending to have been
robbed there.[3]

How far, outside London, the obligation upon the ordinary citizen, under the Statute of Winchester, of helping to
maintain a watch at night, was fulfilled it is difficult to say.
The North Riding records and those of Kesteven and Buckinghamshire contain presentments for not fulfilling this
duty.[4] The watch is mentioned as co-operating with the
magistrates and constables in the election riot at Coventry

[1] *Hertford County Records*, vii. 138. For a favourable view of the constables at
this period see Ogg, ii. 492–4.

[2] Peyton, pp. xlii–xlvi; Gretton, *Oxfordshire Justices of the Peace*, pp. lxii–lxiii;
Clode, ii. 125. The liability of the hundred for riot lasted until 49 & 50 Vic., cap. 38
(1886). S. and B. Webb, *The Parish and the County*, p. 308, n.

[3] *Middlesex Sessions Records, passim; Portledge Papers*, p. 244. The method of
collection seems to have been for one wealthy inhabitant to pay the sum awarded
and for the high constable to levy a rate from the hundred to reimburse him.
Shropshire Quarter Sessions Records, i. 158; *Hertford County Records*, vi, *passim*. Cf.
Nottinghamshire County Records of the Seventeenth Century, passim.

[4] *North Riding Quarter Sessions Records, passim; Buckingham County Records,
passim*. Peyton, pp. lix–lxi and *passim*. The Lancashire magistrates were ordered
by Clarendon in March 1665 to see that watches were duly kept. *H.M.C. Kenyon*,
pp. 75–6.

in 1705.[1] The mention of a guard in connexion with the
Kendal riots of 1696 suggests that some form of watch
organization existed, though it may, of course, have been an
improvisation.[2]

The problem of police was even more complicated in the
increasingly urbanized area comprised by London, Westminster, and their suburbs. It was made harder by the fact
that responsibility was divided between the City authorities,
the Westminster authorities, and the Middlesex justices. An
act of the Common Council of the city of London, passed
in the reign of Charles II, had provided for a body of more
than a thousand bell-men or watchmen to patrol the streets
during the hours of darkness. It further provided that the
inhabitants should perform this duty in person when their
turn came. This force never appears to have been regarded
as at all efficient.[3] More useful, in all probability, was the
beginning of a regular system of street-lighting which likewise dates from the reign of Charles II.[4]

In the areas under the control of the Middlesex justices
an attempt was still being made to police large parts of a
great modern city by the methods prescribed in the statute
of Winchester for the rural England of the middle ages.[5]
Considering that the justices were unable to prevent the
practice of constables hiring paid substitutes to perform their
duties for them, it is not surprising that the problem of
providing an efficient watch proved beyond their powers.[6]

Following complaints on this subject, the Middlesex
sessions made an order in June 1690 requiring petty constables and headboroughs to see that watches were correctly
set by night and wards by day. The watches were to number
twice as many as those usually appointed. This proved
ineffective. In July 1691 the inhabitants of the liberty of
Moorfields complained that a watch was kept only every

---

[1] *Supra*, pp. 49–50.   [2] *Supra*, pp. 102–3.

[3] Macaulay, i. 376; W. M. L. Lee, *A History of Police in England*, 1901, p. 133.
In Oct. 1661 the king complained to the lord mayor that the watch was insufficient.
C.S.P. Dom., 1661–2, pp. 123–4.   [4] Macaulay, i. 379.

[5] Dowdell, pp. 23–4. The provost-marshal, who seems to have been held
responsible for preventing crime in the capital, found after the Great Fire that the
task was beyond his powers. *C.S.P. Dom., 1664–5*, pp. 229–30; *1666–7*, p. 528.

[6] Dowdell, p. 19.

other night, so that crime was frequent.[1] One obstacle to efficiency was the fact that under the Statute of Winchester watching could not be enforced in the winter, and the efforts of the justices to enforce winter watching in spite of this failed. An attempt was also made to supplement the amateur watchmen by a system of paid watchmen. This in turn led to complaints that excessive rates were being levied to pay for this service. More effective, probably, was the unofficial action of groups of wealthy neighbours who combined to pay for a professional watch in their districts.[2]

Something appears to have been expected from the watch, for on several occasions when trouble was anticipated we find orders for stricter attention to watch and ward or for the watch to be doubled.[3] In February 1712 the Middlesex justices, reporting to the queen on the disorders in the London streets, announced that this had been done.[4]

The local civilian police officers and their amateur helpers were not, of course, expected to be able to deal with serious rioting. Indeed, the accounts of the riots at Worcester in 1693, at Kendal in 1696, and at Coventry in 1705 show how rapidly the ordinary forces of the law could lose control in the small provincial towns.[5] The account of the disturbances among the weavers in 1697 or of the Sacheverell riots shows this to be equally true of the capital itself.[6]

'It was on the county itself,' remark the joint historians of English local government, 'not on the individual officers, that rested the immemorial obligation of furnishing an armed force, whether as posse comitatus, to put down any resistance to the keeping of the peace, or in the form of the ancient militia to contribute to the defence of the nation.'[7]

This is in accordance with the legal doctrine of the responsibility of all citizens. But the county could not act except through its officers, and one needs no deep knowledge of

---

[1] *Middlesex Sessions Records*, pp. 12–13 and 49.
[2] Dowdell, pp. 23–6.
[3] *C.S.P. Dom.*, *1668–9*, p. 115; *1680–1*, p. 131; *1690–1*, p. 307; *Middlesex Sessions Records, passim.* On 26 May 1668 Pepys was likely to have met 'with a stop for all night at the Constable's watch at Moorgate by a pragmatical constable'. *Diary*, 26 May 1668.   [4] Dowdell, p. 24.
[5] *Supra*, pp. 49–50, 60–1, 102–3.   [6] *Supra*, pp. 51–4, 84–6.
[7] S. and B. Webb, *The Parish and the County*, p. 305.

English administration at this period to realize that this county responsibility implied action by the justices of the peace.[1] It is going too far to say that their action prevented any disturbances accompanying the Glorious Revolution.[2] There was a certain amount of real disorder, as we have seen; but the ease of the transition to the new régime was doubtless due largely to this source of permanent power and influence in the counties themselves.

So much was the power of the justices taken for granted that, though nominally agents of the central government, they continued their work without waiting for new commissions, unsatisfactory though this was. On 15 May 1689 Shrewsbury wrote to the commissioners of the Great Seal to inquire as to the cause of the delay in issuing their commissions—a delay which the king looked upon as prejudicial to his affairs at a time when so much was happening which was likely to disturb the peace of the kingdom.[3]

How far their independence could be maintained is a difficult problem. In Charles's reign there were many complaints against them, and especially against urban magistrates for lukewarmness in executing the laws against dissenters.[4] We have noted occasional reluctance to assist in providing recruits for the forces. There are even instances of refusals to help tax-collectors.[5]

Normally, however, a real control was exercised over the justices. Their decisions in general or petty sessions were subject to King's Bench. They were directed to reserve difficult cases for the judges on circuit, and all civil functionaries were required to appear at the assizes. 'Finally', we are told, 'the King's Privy Council could either through the Judges on their periodical assizes, or directly through the Custos Rotulorum, at any time issue peremptory instructions for the execution and even for the supplementing of the statutes and common law in whatever way the public

---

[1] In the case of the Surrey justices, for instance, 'the beginnings of a riot seem to have been the one matter which called for rapid action'. H. Jenkinson, introduction to the Surrey records, p. xxxv.

[2] As is done by Trotter, p. 202.

[3] *C.S.P. Dom.*, *1689–90*, p. 105.

[4] Ibid., *1671*, p. 15 and *passim*; *1681–2*, p. 506 and *passim*.

[5] L. M. Marshall, p. 635.

welfare made necessary.'[1] To the activity of the privy council as it concerned the preservation of order we must refer again, but of action through the judges on circuit there is little evidence. In June 1695, however, the lords justices gave special instructions to Baron Turton, whose circuit included Lancashire, to look out for signs of disturbance and to exhort to the strict performance of their duties the justices of an area still disturbed after the treason trials of the previous year.[2]

How far the justices were popular especially among the lower classes of society is one of those questions the historian of this period would like to be able to answer, without having much prospect of ever being in a position to do so.[3] The preamble of a statute of 1694 recites that in spite of previous acts people indicted for riot, forcible entry, assault and battery, and other crimes have been having their cases removed from the courts of quarter sessions to King's Bench by means of writs of *certiorari*, 'fearing to be deservedly punished where they and their offences are well knowne'. The act, therefore, limits the use of such writs.[4] It is doubtless possible to read into this a fear on the part of alleged law-breakers that the class prejudices of the justices, concerning, for example, such things as the game-laws, would be too strong and that a fairer trial might be expected in London. But this is mere speculation.

Corresponding to the justices were the mayors and aldermen or the other elected officials of the corporate towns, both in their powers, in relation to the central government, and in the range of their activities.[5] It is worth remembering, too, that the connexion between the town authorities and those of the surrounding country-side was an extremely close one, and one which recent history had made even closer.

---

[1] S. and B. Webb, p. 306. The secretary of state was consulted by the lord chancellor about the appointment of justices and also played a considerable part in the selection of sheriffs and deputy lieutenants. M. A. Thomson, *The Secretaries of State, 1681–1782*, 1932, pp. 105–6.   [2] *C.S.P. Dom.*, *1694–5*, pp. 493 and 510.   [3] For a discussion of the justices' attitude to their duties see Peyton, p. lxxviii.

[4] Stats. of Realm, 5 & 6 Will. & Mar., cap. 11. It was made perpetual by 8 & 9 Will. III, cap. 33. An example of its use in a case in 1697 can be found in the *Buckingham County Records*, ii. 118, 129, 140.

[5] e.g. the letter to the bailiffs and justices of Droitwich of 26 July 1694, exhorting them to keep the peace there. P.C. 2. 75, p. 447.

'The process of remodelling the borough', writes a recent historian of the reign of Charles II, 'enabled and encouraged the landed gentry to impose their yoke on the municipal corporations; for they were frequently intruded as mayors or recorders.'[1]

To the extent of the justices' activity any set of local records bears ample witness, but much of it must have been of the nature of rough and ready justice. Few could have had profound knowledge of law and administrative precedent. Evidence of one attempt to remedy this defect comes from Shropshire. In October 1697 the clerk of the peace was ordered to 'buy a book of all statutes made and to buy all Acts hereafter made against every Quarter Sessions'. The money for this was to come out of the fund maintained for relieving maimed soldiers—a fund frequently 'raided' at this period for general county purposes.[2]

As the putting down of a riot would involve force and as the improper use of force even for an end laudable in itself has always been held an offence under English law, it was necessary that the law relating to riot should be well understood by those whose duty it was to administer it. And at this period the law relating to riot and allied offences was far from clear and was in fact undergoing a process of development—a process which was to culminate in the Riot Act of 1716, the basis of the modern law on the subject.[3]

The reason for this was the disappearance of the court of Star Chamber, which had been largely occupied in supplementing the deficiencies in the common law in the matter of disturbances of the public peace. The common-law distinction between felony and misdemeanour made it sometimes difficult adequately to punish rioters and limited the power of

---

[1] Ogg, ii. 518. It was the town magistrate, it should be noted, who had been most ready to obstruct action against dissenters. Granted the correctness of Charles's policy towards them, his action was not wholly unjustified.

[2] *Shropshire Quarter Sessions Records*, i. 169. Cf. *Kesteven Quarter Sessions Proceedings*, p. 232. Reresby refused to be sworn for some time 'to avoid trouble as well as to gain time to study the statute law'. *Reresby Memoirs*, p. 98.

[3] For a contemporary account of the duties of the justices with regard to riots see J. Bond, *A Complete guide for Justices of the Peace*, 1695, chap. lxxxv, 'Of Riots, Routs and unlawful Assembleys'. Cf. *Office of the Clerk of Assize*, pp. 51 and 128. On 20 Dec. 1711 the house of commons set up a committee to inquire into the law relating to riots. *C.J.* xvii. 14.

the justices to put down riots.[1] The result was an attempt throughout the period between 1660 and 1714 to bring rioting within the scope of the treason laws by enlarging the scope of 'constructive treason' to include large-scale rioting, on the precedent of certain decisions of the Tudor period.[2]

In this lies the legal interest of the case of Messenger in 1668. A design to pull down houses of ill fame in London was held by all the judges with one exception, that of Baron Hale, to be treason on the ground that the design was general in its object and not confined to the personal grievances of the rioters.[3] Hale's contention had been

'that there was no treason in the case because he said that the Stat. 1 Queen Mary, cap. 12 is that if any persons to the number of twelve or more, assemble to the intent to pull down Inclosures etc. with force, and continue together an hour after proclamation made for their departure, it shall be felony, and if those actions had been treason at common law it had been no purpose to make it felony.'[4]

The principle which guided the majority decision in Messenger's case was successfully appealed to in the cases of Dammaree and Purchase arising out of the Sacheverell riots.[5] The fact that neither of them actually suffered any penalty may have helped to show the inadequacy of the law in this matter and so to pave the way for the Riot Act.

In the matter of the procedure to be followed for suppressing riots the judges in Messenger's case quoted

'a resolution of all the Judges of 39 Eliz. that any Justice of the Peace, Sheriff, or other Magistrate or any other subject of the King, may by the Common Law, arm themselves to suppress Riots, Rebellions, or resist Enemies, and endeavour themselves to suppress such disturbers of the Peace: but they said the most discreet way was for everyone to attend and assist the Justices in such case or other ministers of the King in doing it.'[6]

---

[1] Holdsworth, viii. 328. For Star Chamber's action in regard to riots, &c., ibid. v. 197 ff. The influence of Star Chamber was felt in the further development of the law on this matter, for instance in the definition of an 'unlawful assembly' and in the decision that three was the minimum number of persons who could commit the offence of riot. Ibid. viii. 325–6, 329.

[2] Idid., p. 319.   [3] *Supra*, p. 30; *State Trials*, ii. 583–90.

[4] Ibid., p. 587. The other judges appear to have had the authority of an act of 13 Elizabeth and of a resolution of the judges in a case of 1597. Ibid., p. 589; Holdsworth, loc. cit.

[5] *State Trials*, viii. 219–67 and 552–7.   [6] Ibid. ii. 589–90.

In view of the doubtful extent of the common-law powers of a single justice in this respect, the normal procedure appears to have been action by two justices under the statute 13 Henry IV, cap. 7, with the aid of the sheriff and the posse comitatus, in pursuance of the act 17 Richard II. It is to these two statutes that the council invariably refers when exhorting the local authorities to action.[1] Furthermore, the act provided that when it was not executed the two justices next to the place should forfeit £100 each and other justices of the county in whom there was any default should likewise be fined.[2] Ordinary citizens refusing to assist the sheriff and justices, when suppressing a riot under this act, were liable to imprisonment and fine. Corporations which allowed riots to proceed might be fined or deprived of their franchises.[3]

More important is the question of the actual efficacy of this method of keeping the peace. It has been generally held that the office of high sheriff at this period was merely a ceremonial one. Some colour is given to this by the large number of warrants issued in this period to the various high sheriffs permitting them to reside outside the counties in which they held office.[4]

Sidney and Beatrice Webb assert that by the end of the century all his functions except the purely ceremonial ones were performed by the under-sheriff, who combined in his person this office with the ancient one of county clerk and who, as a paid professional, held his office continuously under successive high sheriffs.[5] 'The High Sheriff', they write, 'equally ceased during the eighteenth century to be called upon in practice to maintain the peace of the county. In Suffolk in 1695, when riotous mobs had destroyed corn-waggons and stolen the corn, Quarter Sessions directed any

---

[1] A single justice could arrest rioters, or order them to disperse under the statutes 1 Mary, cap. 12, and 1 Eliz., cap. 16. Bond, p. 194. Cf. Peyton, p. xvi.

[2] The special responsibility of the justices nearest the place of the riot was recognized by the council; we get letters to the justices 'near' Northampton, Peterborough, &c. P.C. 2. 75, p. 438. The justices were not above encouraging riots at times, especially those of a political nature. The solicitor-general, Raymond, advised the prosecution of two of them in connexion with the Ely riot of 1710. *Supra*, p. 54, n. 2.   [3] Bond, pp. 195 and 198.

[4] *C.S.P. Dom., Will. & Mar., passim*, especially vol. i.

[5] S. and B. Webb, *The Parish and the County*, p. 289.

Justice, in case of a repetition of such tumults, to "issue out his precept to the Sheriff of the County . . . requiring him forthwith to raise and bring the Posse Comitatus". We have come across no such order or precept to the High Sheriff in subsequent years; the Judges act through the High or Petty Constables, or in later times rely on "the invalids" (army pensioners) or the regular force.'[1]

This, however, is certainly not an accurate description of the procedure during the years 1689–1714, nor was 1695 the last year in which a high sheriff was ordered to exercise his ancient powers for the preservation of the peace.

On at least one occasion since 1688 it had been to the sheriff as well as to the justices of the county that the council's precepts to put down a riot had been issued, that of the riot at Coventry in 1689.[2] After the date mentioned by Mr. and Mrs. Webb there is the whole series of instructions from the council dealing with the riots in the Fen country in 1699 and 1701.[3] The letter of 19 January 1699 to the high sheriff and the justices of the peace of Lincolnshire orders them in particular to execute the statute 13 Henry IV, cap. 7, 'for taking the power of the county upon such occasions'. Similar letters were sent in June. In March letters to the same effect were addressed to the high sheriff and justices of Norfolk, Cambridgeshire, Huntingdonshire, and Northamptonshire, and to the bailiff and justices of the Isle of Ely. In May 1701, when Lincolnshire was again disturbed, the sheriff and justices were ordered by the council to intervene.[4]

It is thus probable that the posse comitatus was still recognized as the force upon which lay, in the first instance, the obligation of preserving the public peace. Its actual utility for this purpose may, however, be doubted, though there is little direct evidence of its conduct in the face of disorder. Where the rioters had popular sympathy on their side the posse could not be relied upon for more than nominal obedience. Such, at least, is the picture given in the account of the Northamptonshire enclosure riot of 1710.[5]

---

[1] S. and B. Webb, p. 488, n.
[2] *Supra*, pp. 76–7.
[3] *Supra*, pp. 78–80.
[4] P.C. 2. 77, pp. 293, 309, 350; 78, p. 208.
[5] *Supra*, p. 77–8.

The local justices do not appear even to have attempted to use their statutory powers to quell the corn-riot at Redbridge in December 1712.[1]

For further evidence of the unreliability of the civil forces it is only necessary to consider the large number of instances in which military help was called for almost immediately on the outbreak of disorder. Regular troops within the county affected could be called upon by the justices, or, it would seem, by the sheriff. Their legal powers of action, unless thus specially summoned to assist, remained for long a debatable point.[2]

The responsibility for summoning the aid of the militia is less clear. In 1693 Wood speaks of the mayor of Worcester raising the militia in order to deal with the corn-riots.[3] The militia troops which arrived at Kendal in June 1696 in order to relieve the improvised guard had no doubt been sent by the lord-lieutenant or his deputies.[4] In 1709 the militia was held in readiness to deal with the Bristol corn-riot.[5] In none of these cases was there time for the central government to intervene. Yet in the last resort the use of troops for the suppression of civil disorder must be a matter of national policy. This aspect requires only brief treatment here.

We have seen the attempts of the central government to hasten the suppression of riots and the punishment of rioters by means of letters from the privy council not only to the justices of the peace, the high sheriffs, and the mayors, but also to the lord-lieutenants of the counties affected. During the whole of the period, indeed, matters affecting public order were discussed by the privy council and in William's absence on campaign by the lords justices. The mainspring of the government's action in this as in other domestic matters was, however, undoubtedly the office of the secretaries of state.

As between the two secretaries there was in this period, as

[1] *Supra*, p. 70.
[2] There are no cases of such independent action in our period, as far as I am aware. The legal issue remained unsettled for the best part of the next century. J. P. de Castro, *The Gordon Riots*, 1926, pp. 72–3 and 101.
[3] *Supra*, p. 61.   [4] *Supra*, pp. 102–3.
[5] J. Latimer, *Annals of Bristol in the Eighteenth Century*, pp. 78–9.

far as domestic affairs were concerned, no formal division of duties.[1] Macaulay writes disparagingly of Trenchard, who held the northern department from March to November 1693 and the southern department from then until his death in April 1695, as being 'little more than a superintendent of police, charged to look after the printers of unlicensed books, the pardon of non-juring congregations and the haunters of treason taverns'.[2] But from one point of view it would be possible to write in this fashion of all the distinguished holders of the office during the period. Indeed, if we were to include under the heading of the preservation of order— as no doubt the secretaries of state of the period would themselves have done—the enormous amount of work in connexion with the unravelling of plots, the suppression of seditious publication, and the control of the movements of suspicious persons, we should have to deal with a mass of material whose mere bulk supplies one explanation of the apparent blindness of the secretaries to economic and social issues.[3] They also had, in William's reign, to supervise the efforts of the justices to disarm the catholic part of the population and other suspects and to confiscate their horses in order to prevent the possibility of a Jacobite rising; though only during the first few months after the Revolution, when armed bands of horsemen were said to be moving in the northern counties, and when there were many reports of the gatherings of the 'disaffected', can the danger from this source be said to have been serious.[4]

In criticizing what may occasionally seem to be a rather absurd over-anxiety on the part of the secretaries, it is necessary to remember the peculiar difficulties under which

---

[1] Thomson, p. 105. Mr. and Mrs. Webb unduly minimize, at least as far as this period is concerned, the activity of the central government. *Statutory Authorities for Special Purposes*, p. 460.   [2] Macaulay, v. 393.

[3] Historians have dealt harshly with the corruption and personal malignity revealed in the prosecution for the 'Lancashire plot' of 1694. (See the introduction to the account of the trials published by the Chetham Society in 1853.) It was, however, only one symptom of a social evil which was encouraged by the administrative methods and even by the legislation of the time—the growth of the trade of informer. The Trumbull papers, *H.M.C. Downshire*, i, are full of the 'information' offered by these people and of fulsome appeals for rewards for their 'services'. Informers and *agents provocateurs* were freely used in the reign of Charles II, e.g. *C.S.P. Dom., 1661–2*, pp. 284, 537.   [4] Ibid., *1689–90, passim*.

they laboured.[1] The various government departments during William's reign were not merely often inefficient but rightly suspected of being centres of corruption and of disaffection towards the régime.[2] Shrewsbury himself failed to discover a suitable secretary; and, making all allowances for his peculiarly pessimistic temperament, it is not surprising to find him writing in July 1695, 'I never yet was a month in business without wishing to be out of it.'[3]

The secretary's orders in connexion with searches for seditious literature and with the arrest and custody of suspects all over the country had to be carried out by the 'king's messengers', or 'messengers-in-ordinary', a body of about forty extremely hard-working individuals who, like other servants of the state in those days, suffered from having their pay continually in arrears.[4]

In dealing with suspects, the secretaries were hampered also by their on the whole scrupulous regard for the law. Arrests on the secretary's warrant certainly bulk very large in the calendars of state papers for the reign of William, and their number each week rises to a very high figure at times of crisis. Nevertheless, administrative expediency was not, we may admit, allowed, except perhaps during the height of the Popish-plot terror, to get the better of the legal right of Englishmen. Habeas Corpus was indeed suspended from February to May 1689,[5] and Abbott's narrative shows the hardships, made worse by the prison conditions of the time, which could be suffered in those months by some one quite unimportant believed to be hostile to the new régime.[6] In July 1690 Carmarthen, the lord president of the council, wrote to the king: 'We have made bold with the Habeas

[1] On the police-work of the secretaries of state in the reign of Charles II see F. M. G. Evans, *The Principal Secretary of State*, 1923, pp. 253–8 and 263–7.

[2] On the commissioners of customs and excise see *C.S.P. Dom., 1694–5*, pp. 179–88. On the admiralty, *H.M.C. Downshire*, i. 473–6.

[3] T. C. Nicholson and A. S. Turberville, *Charles Talbot, Duke of Shrewsbury*, 1930, p. 101.

[4] For lists of the messengers in 1692 and 1702 see *Angliae Notitia*, 17th ed., pp. 132–3, and 20th ed., p. 511. For the rates allowed them for journeys, maintaining prisoners, &c., see *H.M.C. Portland*, iv. 178. For their bills for such work see *C.S.P. Dom., Anne*, ii. 472–3 and *passim*. For their petition for payments due in 1697 see ibid., *1697*, p. 167.

[5] Stats. of Realm, 1 Will. & Mar., caps. 3 and 7; *Parliamentary History*, v. 153–9.

[6] *The Narrative of Richard Abbott* (Chetham Soc.), pp. 11–23.

Corpus in securing divers persons and have ordered several more to be secured.' Conditions, however, rapidly returned to normal. In February of the following year the council were advised by the lord chief justice not to make certain arrests upon the confession of Lord Preston, as the persons so arrested would sue for their Habeas Corpus and come out in three days.[1] In June 1692 Nottingham, then secretary of state, ordered Colonel Gibson, commander at Portsmouth, to obey a Habeas Corpus for the removal of a prisoner of his to London and to obey also if he should receive a Habeas Corpus in the future.[2]

The secretary's power of searching printing-houses was challenged after the expiry of the Licensing Act in 1695.[3] In this and in the following year it was contended unsuccessfully in connexion with the escape of Sir James Montgomery that the secretary had no power of commitment in virtue of his office and that a messenger's house could not be held to be a legal prison.[4] The Jacobites also managed to use the time gained by such legal fencing to remove material witnesses for the Crown.[5]

As we have seen, the activity of the Jacobite plotters, like that of the republican extremists in the reign of Charles II, resulted in very little actual disorder. From our point of view the secretary of state has a different importance, as being the link between the civil and the military authorities. The office of secretary of state was intimately connected with the Crown's control of the militia.[6] Instructions to the regular troops might also be transmitted, either directly to him, or through the secretary-at-war.[7] Captain Wroth received orders to intervene in the Northamptonshire riot of 1710 from Walpole, who then held the latter office.[8] Nevertheless, in spite of this centralization of authority it is far from easy to determine, in this period, the precise extent

[1] *C.S.P. Dom.*, *1690–1*, pp. 53 and 255.
[2] Ibid., *1691–2*, p. 312.
[3] *H.M.C. Downshire*, i. 593; Evans, loc. cit.
[4] *C.S.P. Dom.*, *1694–5*, v. 493, and vi. 350; *H.M.C. Downshire*, i. 690–1. The case was not by any means clear, and the recorder in deciding for the secretary was described as cutting the Gordian knot of law he could not untie.
[5] *H.M.C. Downshire*, i, *passim*.   [6] Thomson, p. 77.
[7] Ibid., p. 107. For the office of secretary-at-war, ibid., pp. 64–76; Clode, i. 71.
[8] *Supra*, p. 77.

to which either the militia or the regular troops were used for preserving internal order. Every time, however, that large-scale rioting did occur, military aid was requisitioned.[1]

The only historian of the army who has investigated this problem in any detail singles out the period of the Restoration, which saw the beginning of a standing army in this country, as also the period in which regular troops were first used on a large scale for the maintenance of internal order.[2] Apart from those detailed for garrison duty and other particular services the troops were, he says, 'engaged as an armed police for the carrying out of the oppressive laws against dissenters', and in various other such tasks.[3]

At the beginning of Charles's reign it was less clear what proportion of the task of maintaining internal order could and would be entrusted to regular troops. 'For his guard', wrote the Venetian envoy in 1661, 'the King keeps 2,000 foot and 800 horse: not an excessive number but noteworthy by comparison with the way in which past kings used to live, who had no troops of any kind except a few horsemen for show.'[4]

In the early years of the reign the royal guards and other regular troops raised by the king were the key to the problem of security. The Convention parliament proved unwilling to settle the militia.[5] And, when parliamentary difficulties were overcome, the task of organization proved a slow one. In the autumn of 1662, when serious trouble was expected, the Venetian ambassador reported that the army was very strong, consisting of 10,000 combatants, horse and foot, all good troops, as well as the militia. Nevertheless, three new regiments of horse were to be raised out of old loyalists.[6] In November a company of foot and one of horse were sent into the City to forestall an expected disturbance, much to the annoyance of the trained bands, who considered themselves

---

[1] An exception should be made for election riots. According to previous practice, on 5 July 1689 William ordered that all troops, except those in garrisons, should, for the period of the election, leave the town in which they were quartered. This action was repeated on subsequent occasions and the practice was made statutory in the reign of George II. Clode, i. 195, and appendix, no. 5.

[2] Ibid. ii. 125–7.

[3] Ibid. i. 53–5.

[4] *C.S.P. Ven.*, 1661–4, p. 84.

[5] Ranke, iii. 355.

[6] *C.S.P. Ven.*, 1661–4, p. 187.

quite capable of defending the City without assistance.[1] This was to prove only one instance of the constant jealousy of the military felt by the City authorities in this reign and of their reluctance to submit to supervision by them of their security measures.[2] Nevertheless in November 1663 the royal troops were again kept under arms in order to prevent trouble in the capital.[3]

In 1665 Coventry suggested to Arlington that the king should consider raising more troops to cope with internal disorder.[4] There was even a suggestion made that the county militia, though not the London trained bands, should be abolished and that the people would be willing to be taxed instead to provide a regular force.[5] But although there were several occasions in the following years when regular troops were used, especially in the capital, for the suppression of riots, the keeping of internal order became more and more the prime task of the militia. And it was the militia rather than the regular army which was to the fore in enforcing the repressive measures against the dissenters.

The distribution of the regular troops rendered their use for the maintenance of internal order a matter of some difficulty. Apart from the royal guards at Westminster, the very important garrison of the Tower, and some troops of horse scattered through six or eight towns in the south-east and the north, the regular army consisted of infantry stationed in the coastal forts.[6] Suggestions were occasionally made that other garrisons should be set up. In 1663, for instance, it was suggested that one at Chepstow would enable the four neighbouring counties to be overawed, they being far from any other garrison and weak in militia.[7] Clifford also valued highly the ability of this very scattered army to repress disturbances and suggested in 1670 that the king would be advised to strengthen the forts and to increase the numbers of men in them before announcing his conversion. He also suggested the creation of some new citadels, among the places mentioned being Yarmouth and Bristol, two noted

---

[1] Ibid., pp. 204–5.
[2] e.g. *C.S.P. Dom.*, *1671*, p. 356, and *1680–1*, p. 131.
[3] *C.S.P. Ven.*, *1661–4*, p. 267.   [4] *C.S.P. Dom.*, *1664–5*, p. 508.
[5] Ibid., *1665–6*, pp. xxxvii–xxxviii.
[6] Ibid., *1673–5*, pp. 490–4.   [7] Ibid., *1663–4*, p. 359.

centres of nonconformity.[1] But the idea that the country
could be held down for long by regular troops was only held
in extreme court circles. The duke of York was reported
in 1676 to have talked of the necessity of having guards to
put down tumults,[2] but the government wisely refrained
from using the army for this purpose more than was strictly
necessary. Although the guards had been used to put down
the rioting seamen in 1666, and the apprentices in the more
dangerous affair of 1668, in dealing with the weavers' riots of
1675 considerable reluctance was shown to taking the matter
out of the hands of the London trained bands.[3] As we have
seen, no caution could prevent the fear of the army from playing its part in the political convulsions of the next few years.

It is not always easy to discover, when troops are mentioned as dealing with disturbances, whether the regulars
or the militia are meant. In dealing with the post-Revolu-
tion period there is again the difficulty of finding out where
exactly troops were quartered. There were still, of course,
large bodies at the Tower, Portsmouth, and Plymouth, and,
in addition to the coastal strongholds, garrisons at York,
Chester, and Carlisle. From 1660 to 1692, the Crown had
in addition no statutory facilities for the movement of troops
from one part of the kingdom to another. Clode believed
this to have been an intentional limitation intended to force
the king to keep the troops in the garrisons. But although
conditions changed after the act of 1692, and the practice
grew up of moving the troops from time to time to new
quarters so that no intimacy between them and the people
might grow up, troop movements in this period are difficult
to trace.[4] All the documents relating to the quartering
of troops refer to the early years of William's reign,[5] but
there is no reason for believing that the impression which
they give of concentration along the coast or around the
capital would be untrue of later parts of our period, though

---

[1] Hartmann, pp. 153–4 and 220.
[2] *Hatton Correspondence*, i. 129.   [3] *C.S.P. Dom., 1675–6*, pp. 250–63.
[4] Clode, p. 217; Stats. of Realm, 4 Will. & Mar., cap. 13.
[5] S.P. Dom., King William's Chest, 5, no. 129; 10, nos. 127 and 131. The first
of these is 'a list of forces necessary in garrisons in time of peace'. A document among
those for 1695 (ibid. 15, no. 105) also gives a list of quarters, but from internal
evidence it must belong to the previous reign.

doubtless troops were quartered elsewhere when occasion arose. In September 1693 troops were quartered in Norwich and in certain places in Huntingdonshire and Northampton-shire.[1] There seems no evidence of their having taken part in the suppression of the corn-riots which occurred in the latter county in that year, though, as we have seen, troops were sent to deal with the Northamptonshire enclosure riots in 1710.[2] If we consider the garrison duty which had to be performed, the numbers of regular troops were never large. In 1689 there were in England about 17,000 soldiers, of whom about 7,000 were Dutch.[3] The figure for English troops appears to have remained fairly constant, from ten to twelve thousand, while the numbers of Dutch rose.[4] The constant attempts in parliament to limit the numbers of the troops belongs to the political history of the reign. After the peace of Ryswick, when the Dutch guards were sent back, there were nearly 15,000 troops on the English establish-ment, a figure which parliament made William halve.[5] The renewal of the war caused a large increase in the numbers of troops employed, but after the peace of Utrecht the internal forces were reduced to 8,000 men.[6]

A knowledge of the use and organization of the militia, in this period, is fundamental to a correct understanding of the problem of order, and it is to be regretted that the com-parative military insignificance of the institution should have led to its neglect by historians of the army.[7] This has meant that several problems connected with it cannot as yet be clearly answered.[8]

[1] C.S.P. Dom., 1693, pp. 317 and 337. In June of that year a troop of dragoons had been quartered in Romney and its neighbourhood to patrol the roads, doubtless for smugglers and Jacobites. Ibid., p. 175.

[2] Supra, p. 77. Troops were regularly stationed at Oundle in the eighteenth century (V.C.H. Northampton, iii. 88). This may have suggested their use, if such was already the case in 1710.   [3] S.P. King William's Chest, 5, nos. 12 and 129.

[4] For 1691 and 1692, ibid., 10, no. 124; 13, nos. 12 and 15.

[5] Walton, p. 497.   [6] Clode, pp. 259–60.

[7] See Ogg, i. 252–3, for an account of it from the military point of view. For an example of the composition and training of a town militia see Latimer, Annals of Bristol in the Eighteenth Century, pp. 79–80.

[8] The method of co-operation between the civil authorities and the lieutenancy, for instance, is far from clear. It seems to have varied with the urgency of the occa-sion. Within the hundred the same officers, the chief constables, represented both. Peyton, p. xlii.

As we have seen, the first years of the reign were largely occupied with the reorganization of the militia with a view to bringing it up to strength, and to eliminating disloyal elements from among its officers.[1] This was the more necessary in that the disbanding of large portions of the old army presented political and administrative problems of great delicacy.[2]

In the years 1661–3 the militia were called out in several counties to prevent disturbances. In some counties, notably Yorkshire and Westmorland, it was found necessary to supplement them by regiments of loyalist volunteers. An entire regiment was formed in Yorkshire, early in 1664, out of the nobility and gentry of that county.[3] Meanwhile, the London trained bands, whose effectiveness had been proved in the civil war, and who were to be prominent on several occasions in the new reign, had rapidly been brought into condition. In May 1661 no fewer than 20,000 of them, 'all fine fellows of good appearance', were reviewed in the park by the king. Elsewhere there was considerable delay in the work, and there were complaints, particularly from the south-western counties, that the enemies of the king were being encouraged by the disarray of the militia.[4] By 1666 these preliminary difficulties appear to have been overcome. In July when an invasion was anticipated, after the Great Fire when there were fears of widespread disorder, and again when a rebellion broke out in Scotland, the militia came out in large numbers and good order.[5]

It would be tedious to recount the number of occasions when the militia were employed to keep order in the later years of the reign. In London, where they were constantly called upon, their most notable employment was the suppression of the weavers' riots in August 1675, though on this occasion one or two officers were alleged to have refused their assistance.[6] In June 1676 the musters of the City

---

[1] *C.S.P. Dom., Charles II, passim; C.S.P. Ven., 1659–61, passim.*

[2] Ibid., p. 204.

[3] *C.S.P. Dom., 1661–2,* pp. 92, 155–6, 182, 551; *1663–4,* p. 332; *C.S.P. Ven., 1661–4,* p. 283.

[4] *C.S.P. Dom., 1661–2,* p. 430; *1663–4,* pp. 150–5, 286–7, 352, 381–2, 645.

[5] Ibid., *1666–7,* pp. xi, xx–xxii, 127, 168; *H.M.C. le Fleming,* p. 42.

[6] *Middlesex County Records,* iv. 62.

trained bands were taken, and the total number given as
8,351.[1] The tendencies to slackness latent in unprofessional
forces became harder to control as times grew less troubled,
and the lieutenancy was forced in September 1679, when
disorder again threatened, to issue instructions that defaulters
should be severely dealt with.[2]

With the problem of order in mind, it is not hard to see
why the question of the control of the militia should, before
the end of the reign, have again become a subject of controversy between the king and his parliament.[3] And the
control of the militia was not unnaturally among the primary
objects of his successor.[4]

If, apart from their use in London, there is little direct
evidence of reliance upon the regular troops for maintaining
order under William III or Anne, the same is not true
of the militia. This latter force, which had the advantage
from the government's point of view of being less suspect
to that section of public opinion which could be voiced in
parliament, was the real key to the problem of order. The
early months of the reign of William and Mary found the
militia again in a poor state of preparedness, owing perhaps
to the various political crises through which the country
had recently passed.[5] Steps were soon taken to remedy this,
at least as far as the important militias of London and
Middlesex were concerned.[6] In a document, probably of
1690, the number of the militia for the country as a whole
was given as 92,868, of whom 6,000 were mounted. The
London trained bands then contributed 9,000 men and 6,000
auxiliaries, and the two regiments of foot comprising the
trained bands of the Tower Hamlets amounted to 1,920 men.[7]

[1] C.S.P. Dom., 1676-7, p. 164.   [2] Ibid., 1679-80, p. 253.
[3] On the parliamentary debates on this see H.M.C. Ormonde, N.S. iv, pp. xix,
475, 485-6.   [4] Reresby Memoirs, passim.
[5] See Col. Mildmay's speech in the house of commons on 15 Mar. 1688/9 on the
occasion of the Ipswich mutiny, exhorting the king to settle the militia, and especially
that of London. A. Grey, Debates, ix. 169. On the condition of the militia in
Lancashire and the north in the summer of 1689 see C.S.P. Dom., 1689-90,
pp. 150, 168, 219. See also Grey, p. 268.
[6] C.S.P. Dom., 1689-90, p. 335; 1690-1, pp. 14, 57, 65-6; H.M.C. Portland,
ii. 163. For the Cornish militia, supra, p. 109. Col. Mildmay had estimated the
number as 150,000.
[7] S.P. King William's Chest, 8, no. 51. The invasion scares of the first three years

On public holidays and popular anniversaries throughout these reigns, and on other occasions when trouble was expected, the trained bands of London and the Tower Hamlets were still called upon to provide guards and patrols.[1] For this activity the secretary of state was at least on some occasions responsible.[2]

We have already dealt at some length with the use of the troops and the trained bands to suppress the riots against the provost-marshals in 1695, and the weavers' riots of 1689 and 1697.[3] An account of the Sacheverell riots, and of the measures taken to put them down and to prevent their recurrence, would also show the importance attached to this section of the militia, although it was the dispatch of the guards by the queen on the night of March 1 that was the decisive action.[4]

In the country districts, where there were probably no regular troops within reach, the importance of the militia as a means of preventing possible turbulence among the poorer classes must have been even greater.[5] We have mentioned its use at Worcester in 1693 and at Kendal in 1696. On other occasions the central government intervened by means of letters from the privy council to the lord-lieutenants, ordering them to assist the civil authorities in

of the reign led to the calling out of the militia in many areas. For Derbyshire in 1689–90 see Cox, i. 183; for Huntingdonshire in 1690 see *H.M.C. Manchester*, p. 66. For activity in the southern counties in 1692 see Luttrell, ii. 443 ff. In 1690 and 1692 indemnity acts were needed to cover breaches of the law involved in the excessive activity of the militia. Stats. of Realm, 2 Will. & Mar., Sess. 2, caps. 12 and 13; 4 Will. & Mar., cap. 19. See also Walton, pp. 468–505.

[1] e.g. *C.S.P. Dom.*, *1697*, p. 16; *Hatton Correspondence*, ii. 176; *Portledge Papers*, pp. 224, 232; State Papers, Queen Anne, 20, nos. 2 and 5; Luttrell, vi. 709.

[2] Thomson, p. 107.

[3] *Supra*, pp. 83–6 and 116–17.

[4] *Supra*, pp. 51–3 and references there, especially Luttrell, vi, and *State Trials*, viii. 224. In November 1711 they were called out again to prevent whig demonstrations against the peace. *Wentworth Papers*, pp. 211–13.

[5] The relations between the regular troops and the militia, when used for such purposes, is not clear. Reresby in 1682, as governor of York and commander of the garrison, achieved not without difficulty his wish that the militia should be under his command 'in case of tumults and insurrections, or on other occasions when I should have need of them for his Majesty's service'. *Reresby Memoirs*, p. 261. Similar problems constantly arose; see, e.g., *C.S.P. Dom.*, *1663–4*, p. 340, for a dispute at Kingston.

restoring and maintaining order. Such letters were sent
to the lord-lieutenant of Lincolnshire in connexion with the
disturbances among the fenmen in 1699 and 1701, and to
the lord-lieutenant of Cornwall about the Truro corn-riot
of 1700.[1]

[1] P.C. 2. 75, pp. 146–7; 77, pp. 293 and 439; 78, p. 208.

CONCLUSION

THE half-century which we have chronicled was one of rapid change, and the main interest of the narrative shifts from decade to decade. The study of the popular disturbances of the time illumines now one section and now another of the nation's life. Our attention has been drawn first of all to tumults whose origin springs from those revolutionary movements in church and state which had been thrown up during the stresses of the Interregnum. Although some of the economic disturbances with which we have had to deal fall within the reign of Charles II, the major events of the period belong to the political sphere. The same is even more markedly true of his successor's short and disturbed tenure of the throne.

In the reign of William III, in spite of the continual plots of the Jacobite faction and of the long spells of warfare abroad, the disharmonies in the economic and social life of the country become far more apparent. To discuss how far this was due to changes in the general social and economic structure of England, how far to the particular financial stress imposed by the wars, and how far, finally, to the accidental circumstances of a run of bad harvests would take us far beyond the boundaries set by our subject. For the reign of Anne there are similar questions which await answer. But in her reign there is a notable lessening of overt social conflict, in part compensated for by the acerbity of party struggles.

One source of trouble unites the whole period, the difficulty of securing recruits for the armed forces and the constant friction between the military on the one hand and the civilian population on the other. And it is on this aspect of the subject that the reign of Anne not unnaturally throws most light. It is clear that there were enough disturbances, and enough potentially disorderly elements in the population, for the whole question to be one which, at least in its administrative aspect, had to be faced by every government of the period. Neither in London nor in rural England could the civil power unassisted be relied upon for the maintenance of the public peace. On the other hand, we have found very little evidence to substantiate the theory that the key to the problem was the existence of a standing army. The assumption that the governments of the second half of the century could afford to drop the social paternalism of their predecessors because the availability of regular troops did away with all fears of a popular rising has a certain plausibility. But it is one which it is only possible to maintain on a long-range view of the facts. Except on very rare occasions, the regular army played no part in maintaining order, and any attempt to extend its use would have resulted in widespread discontent.

In the counties, indeed, the medieval expedient of summoning the posse comitatus had not wholly been abandoned. But this point should not be pressed too far. Where, as was often the case, the mass of the population was in sympathy with the rioters, this was unlikely to be effective. As soon as the mob had passed out of the control of the constables, there remained only the militia. Officered by men of the same type as the civil administrators of the county, and including the stable and propertied men of the county, it had a real interest in preventing the extension of disorder. It was the natural ally of the hard-pressed mayor or justice. The importance which, as we know from the political conflicts of the time, was attached to the militia by contemporary statesmen is shown to be fully justified by the records of its activities drawn from administrative sources.

When we pass from the administrative to the social aspects of the subject, generalization becomes more difficult. Indeed, the most obvious impression which the period leaves on the mind is one of variety. When we run through the list of the major disturbances it is obvious that we are dealing with a society in an advanced stage of economic and social differentiation, and one which no formula can adequately cover. We have, it is true, confirmed the belief that there was in this period no movement for social revolution or even social reform, based upon the class consciousness of the poorer sections of the population. Whatever communistic elements in society and thought had existed during the Interregnum vanished with surprising swiftness

after the Restoration. The deeper reasons for this fall outside our scope, nor is it possible here to discuss the problem
of how far religious and even scientific speculation replaced
questionings as to the nature of society itself. Of the fact
of the change the proofs we have adduced seem amply
sufficient—the silence of contemporary writers and the unwillingness of the administration to pay attention to any
popular outbreaks that could not be connected with the
political opposition.

Nothing lends itself less easily to description and analysis
than that complex of habits and prejudices, ambitions and
fears, which moulds the social thinking of a ruling class.
But the lack of any real movement for social change must
be taken into account, as well as the growing wealth of the
country, when we consider the feeling of security which
seems to have prevailed among the English ruling classes
in this period. And it is this which perhaps explains the
leniency with which isolated disturbances were on the whole
treated, when compared with the ferocity shown by the same
class towards their social inferiors in the times of the Tudors
and the early Stuarts.

For there was, it seems, considerable agitation about
certain of the economic, social, and political phenomena
of the period, more, perhaps, than historians have generally
realized. These protests were still animated by the belief that
what was necessary was a restoration of the old governmental
control over economic activity and social life. Although it is
true that such disturbances were on the whole more numerous during the latter half of our period, this does not prove
that the cessation of such control was something new following upon the Revolution. The process by which central
control was relaxed was a gradual one, and the disturbances
show merely that the policy of complete surrender to the
economic forces of the new age had not yet been whole-
heartedly accepted by their victims. Nor, apparently, did
they accept the view that their misfortunes were almost
entirely the result of their own moral failings.

We have examined the protests of dwellers in corn-
growing areas against the transport of corn to centres where
it could command a higher price than they could afford to

pay. We have noted how the cloth-weavers of Worcester
reacted to the decay of their monopoly, the framework
knitters to unemployment brought about by disregard of
the old rules of apprenticeship, and the London silk-weavers
to the competition of cheap Asiatic labour. In each case we
are dealing with protests of an essentially conservative nature.
The government is still thought of as something outside
economic conflicts, something which can still intervene to
restore the just balance of society. Only in a state so regu-
lated would it be possible once again for the different classes
to carry on their affairs in security. Where these discontents,
stimulated by some particular local hardship, or affecting
some element of the population psychologically ripe for
violence, broke into open disorder, the rioting which ensued
was animated by no common aim beyond that of immediate
revenge upon the nearest personification of the people's
enemies, a corn-dealer, an excise-man, or an East India
merchant. Into a world economically overshadowed by the
East India Company and the London money-market, busy
evolving the greatest instrument of its domination, the Bank
of England, the riots of this period bring a strange breath
of medievalism. To the flourishing business man or improving farmer, for whom social problems were already a question
of 'rates', just as to the secretaries of state preoccupied with
Jacobite plots, the riots were, what they must seem to the
historian, a painful anachronism.

We are dealing with people whose minds still run along
the old lines, who are still thinking in terms of apprenticeship, local monopoly, fair price, and not of the problems of
full-grown capitalism, wages, hours of labour, cyclic depressions. One fear alone clearly unites this period to a later
one, the fear of technological unemployment.

So, too, the existence of a permanent body of able-bodied
unemployed is, in spite of the numerous workhouse projects
and experiments, looked upon, as in the sixteenth century,
as a question of vagrancy, to be met by penal laws rather
than by remedial measures directed to providing work. But
this side of the question has received so much discussion
that it is unnecessary to pursue it, once it has been placed
within its context.

Similarly, the problems presented by the growth of the metropolis and the simultaneous growth there of a vast semi-pauper, semi-criminal population of unmanageable proportions shading by ill-defined degrees into an industrial proletariat of rapidly increasing economic and moral degradation were thought of, when thought of at all, in the terms of an earlier age. Efforts were still being made to check the growth of the City by legislation against new buildings, of which the only effect could be the increase of that overcrowding of whose inevitable consequences the Great Plague had given unmistakable warning. The task of devising a system of local government for the metropolitan area, which would achieve at least the prevention of crime and the establishment of minimum sanitary standards, was a task beyond the imagination of an age so rich in innovation in other spheres.

The blindness to social problems of the ruling classes during this intensely acquisitive age, and its connexion with economic and religious doctrine, have provided a theme for many writers. Our questions must be directed rather to inquiring whether the acceptance of their condition by the victims of this blindness was indeed widespread, or whether by concentrating on instances of protest we have not overestimated the social evils of the time. We have been taught that it is not the populations which are the most downtrodden that revolt against the hardships of their lot. We may ask whether the absence of social discontent in this period meant in fact that conditions were on the whole as good as they had been, and were perhaps improving with the general rise in the prosperity of the country, or whether they were so bad as to render the working-classes too hopeless even to attempt their own betterment. What, for instance, is the significance of the acceptance by the rural population almost without protest of the increasingly severe game-laws whose administration by those most interested in their maintenance was ultimately to do so much to embitter class feeling?[1]

Our introductory chapter has shown some of the difficulties which confront any one who attempts to answer

[1] S. and B. Webb, *The Parish and the County*, pp. 597–9; Chambers, pp. 74–5.

these questions. And the fact, emphasized more than once, that conditions differed vastly in different areas suggests that progress towards their ultimate solution is only possible along the lines of local history.

From the point of view prevalent, however, at Whitehall and in the city of London, the country was one. It was a unitary state battling for its rightful place among the nations of Europe in an age when economic and social welfare were subordinated to considerations of power politics. For large portions of our period and for almost the whole of its latter half, war is the dominant factor in national politics and in the evolution, economic and perhaps social, of the nation.

One is tempted therefore to ask how far the attitude of the common people towards the wars is illustrated in the foregoing pages. Evidence of widespread belief in their necessity is not forthcoming. The second Dutch war had at its outbreak a certain amount of popularity. But the wars against France would appear to have been supported only by very limited classes. Outside their ranks—the ranks of the whigs —there was, at the most, indifference. The squires grumbled at taxation and the common people strove to rescue their friends and neighbours from the clutches of the press-gang and recruiting agent. If it was the tories rather than the whigs for whom the populace was ready to riot, their identification with the peace party must be held at least partly responsible.

Apart from this we have not advanced to any great degree our knowledge of the political activities of the mob. Its use by unscrupulous party leaders was the natural corollary of the wider interest taken in political issues, and of the increasing value set upon a seat in parliament. Its successful use depended only on a clear understanding of certain very simple prejudices. But in the last resort the riotous election mob of the eighteenth century depended upon the existence in the towns of a stratum of population uninterested in maintaining standards of civic order and prepared to break a few windows and even heads, if encouraged by a liberal distribution of free drink.

The problem of the urban mob was one of the social

problems handed on by this age to its successors. But together with these problems it failed to hand on a technique for their solution, nor was the society of the early eighteenth century one particularly fitted for the purpose of finding one. With the humanitarian achievements which stand to the credit of many private individuals in the next century, and even to the credit of some of those engaged in local government, it would be unjust to pronounce too sweeping a judgement on the age. But the period of the later Stuarts affords little material for those who believe that the responsibility for the social welfare of the population rests to a large degree on the shoulders of the central government. Energy, foresight, and the spirit of adventure were qualities not lacking in English society at the turn of the seventeenth and eighteenth centuries, but they were qualities which were being placed more and more wholly at the service of individual profit.

restoring and maintaining order. Such letters were sent to the lord-lieutenant of Lincolnshire in connexion with the disturbances among the fenmen in 1699 and 1701, and to the lord-lieutenant of Cornwall about the Truro corn-riot of 1700.[1]

[1] P.C. 2. 75, pp. 146–7; 77, pp. 293 and 439; 78, p. 208.

APPENDIX

Prices of wheat, 1660–1714; annual average price
of wheat per imperial quarter at Eton.[1]

				s.	*d.*					*s.*	*d.*
1660	–	–	–	51	8	1688	–	–	–	42	1
1661	–	–	–	64	1	1689	–	–	–	27	6
1662	–	–	–	67	9	1690	–	–	–	31	8
1663	–	–	–	52	3	1691	–	–	–	31	1
1664	–	–	–	37	1	1692	–	–	–	42	8
1665	–	–	–	45	2	1693	–	–	–	61	11
1666	–	–	–	33	0	1694	–	–	–	58	7
1667	–	–	–	33	0	1695	–	–	–	48	6
1668	–	–	–	36	7	1696	–	–	–	65	0
1669	–	–	–	40	7	1697	–	–	–	55	0
1670	–	–	–	38	1	1698	–	–	–	62	7
1671	–	–	–	38	6	1699	–	–	–	58	7
1672	–	–	–	37	6	1700	–	–	–	36	7
1673	–	–	–	42	8	1701	–	–	–	34	5
1674	–	–	–	62	10	1702	–	–	–	26	11
1675	–	–	–	59	2	1703	–	–	–	33	0
1676	–	–	–	34	9	1704	–	–	–	42	7
1677	–	–	–	38	6	1705	–	–	–	27	6
1678	–	–	–	54	0	1706	–	–	–	23	9
1679	–	–	–	55	0	1707	–	–	–	26	1
1680	–	–	–	41	3	1708	–	–	–	37	11
1681	–	–	–	42	8	1709	–	–	–	71	11
1682	–	–	–	40	3	1710	–	–	–	71	6
1683	–	–	–	36	7	1711	–	–	–	49	6
1684	–	–	–	40	3	1712	–	–	–	42	5
1685	–	–	–	42	8	1713	–	–	–	46	9
1686	–	–	–	31	1	1714	–	–	–	46	1
1687	–	–	–	23	0						

[1] From R. E. Prothero (Lord Ernle), *English Farming Past and Present*, 1912, p. 440 (Messrs. Longmans, Green & Co., Ltd.).

INDEX